Promise Keeper

A mother's beautiful story
from tears of loss
to triumph and a promise kept

by Elise Pappas

Promise Keeper

Copyright © 2020 by Star Label Publishing

Published by Star Label Publishing
P.O. Box 1511, Buderim, QLD, Australia
publishing@starlabel.com.au
Editor and Interior: Rebecca Moore
Cover art and design: Tony Moore

1st Edition September, 2020
All rights reserved. No part of this publication may be reproduced in any form; stored in a retrieval system; or transmitted; or used in any other form; or by any other means without prior written permission of the publisher (except for brief quotes for the purpose of review or promotion).

Scripture quotations marked (NIV) are taken from the Holy Bible, New International Version®, NIV®. Copyright © 1973, 1978, 1984, 2011 by Biblica, Inc.™ Used by permission of Zondervan. All rights reserved worldwide. www.zondervan.com. The "NIV" and "New International Version" are trademarks registered in the United States Patent and Trademark Office by Biblica, Inc.™

Scripture quotations marked (NLT) are taken from the *Holy Bible, New Living Translation,* copyright © 1996, 2004, 2007, 2013 by Tyndale House Foundation. Used by permission of Tyndale House Publishers, Inc., Carol Stream, Illinois 60188. All rights reserved.

Scripture quotations from *The Message*. Copyright © by Eugene H. Peterson 1993, 1994, 1995, 1996, 2000, 2001, 2002. Used by permission of Tyndale House Publishers, Inc.

Scripture quotations marked (AMP) are taken from *The Amplified® Bible*, Copyright © 2015 by The Lockman Foundation. Used by permission. (www.Lockman.org.) All rights reserved.

All other copyrighted material contained herein referenced at source.

The views expressed here-in remain the sole responsibility of the author, who exempts the publisher from all liability. The author and publisher do not assume responsibility for any loss, damage, or disruption caused by the contents, errors or omissions, whether such contents, errors or omissions result from opinion, negligence, accident, or any other cause, and hereby disclaim any and all liability to any party.

ISBN: 978-0-6484602-4-4

To my adoring husband Daniel –

thank you for your steadfast love,

and to our beautiful children,

Jonathan and Sophie.

CONTENTS

Foreword		vii
Introduction		1
1.	Saying Yes to Jesus	3
2.	A Whole New World	7
3.	The Proposal	13
4.	The Diagnosis	19
5.	Arabella	25
6.	Purpose in your Pain	33
7.	Fruit in the Desert	39
8.	Perseverance	49
9.	Holding Pattern	55
10.	New Wine Calls for a New Wineskin	61
11.	A Double Blessing	67
12.	The Scare	73
13.	Bow Once	79
14.	IVF	91

15.	From Small Things, Big Things Grow	101
16.	Come With Me	105
17.	The Power of Saying Yes	111
18.	Trust in the Process	121
19.	How's Your Faith?	125
20.	Spoils of War	131
21.	New Life	137
22.	A Canvas of Grace	141
Appendices		147
Notes		153
About the Author		155

FOREWORD

Then Jesus answered and said to her, "O woman, great is your faith! Let it be to you as you desire." And her daughter was healed from that very hour. (Matthew 15:28 NKJV)

One of the statements that strikes us in the new testament is this one: *"woman great is your faith"*.

How amazing that Jesus stops and takes the time to publicly honour this woman because of her persistence in standing firmly to believe for her daughter's healing and deliverance.

We all go through situations in life where our faith is tested; where we come against what looks like an impossible obstacle. Elise's story is one like this. While facing what impossible odds, she clung tightly even in the midst of grief and loss, believing that one day she would see *"the goodness of God in the land of the living"*.

God is looking for this same faith in His children again today. The Bible says in 2 Corinthians 1:20 that *"All Gods promises are Yes and amen"* however, sadly not all of us are believing for His promises! Too many of us are living beneath circumstances that God wants to give us victory over.

We do not need to live in hopelessness and defeat. We can choose to have faith in God and see His promises revealed in our lives.

For any person walking through a season where they are trusting and believing God for a miracle this book will show you that it is indeed through "faith and patience" that we inherit the promises of God.

Elise's story so beautifully highlights that hope in God does not disappoint and even though weeping may last for a night, joy comes again in the morning!

In a world that has become increasingly filled with doubt and unbelief, this testimony of faith and hope will put courage and strength in so many to believe for their own breakthrough.

This book needs to get into the hands of EVERY person who is in despair over their current situation. Elise's story carries something the world needs right now...a spirit of faith that will help people everywhere receive their own testimony of triumph over adversity.

Leanne Matthesius
Senior Pastor
Awaken Church

INTRODUCTION

We all have a story worth sharing, and I have always been fascinated by other's stories. Our stories reveal courage, they inspire. They enthuse and serve as a great reminder of God's faithfulness in our lives. Revelation chapter 12 verse 11 (NIV) says that, 'they triumphed over him by the blood of the Lamb and by the word of their testimony'. Our stories, our testimonies, are powerful and for a while now I have felt compelled to write mine down.

David wrote in Psalm chapter 145, verses 5-6 (ERV):

> I will tell about your miracles. People will tell about the amazing things you do and I will tell everyone how great you are.

A friend once said to me that someone who can keep smiling through the trials, challenges and difficulties in life is someone rather special.

My hope and prayer for every single person that picks up *Promise Keeper* is that you are reminded of God's love and faithfulness. We serve such a loving and kind God. That despite whatever difficulty you may be facing, that you would come alive again and be encouraged that His promises never waver. This is not to discount your pain, but to learn to smile regardless. I'm sure this book might make you laugh, it may even make you cry, but amidst it all, I pray it'll bring healing to your life just as writing down these words have brought to mine.

Love Elise x

A song of David.

I will tell of your greatness, my God and King.
I will praise your name forever and ever.
I will praise you every day. I will praise your name forever and ever.
The Lord is great and deserves all our praise!
No one can fully understand his greatness!
Each generation will praise you and tell the next generation about the great things you do.
Your majesty and glory are wonderful.
I will tell about your miracles.
People will tell about the amazing things you do,
and I will tell everyone how great you are.
They will talk about your goodness and sing about your justice.

(Psalm 145 verses 1-7 ERV)

Chapter 1

SAYING "YES" TO JESUS

"For I know the plans I have for you," declares the Lord, "plans to prosper you and not to harm you, plans to give you a hope and a future."
(Jeremiah 29:11)

I always believed in God, had always prayed, and even as a young girl in Sunday School, I remember marking off my Bible reading list, wanting to read through as much of the Bible as I could. But as I grew through high school and university years, I certainly didn't know what it was to have a personal relationship with Jesus. I would pray if something wasn't going right and even call myself a Christian, but I certainly wasn't living for Him.

On the 24th December, 2006 we were holidaying on the Sunshine Coast and, as per normal, we would attend a Christmas Eve service. However, this time I was invited by my cousin to attend the, then called, Kings Christian Church on the Sunshine Coast, which is now

Calvary Christian Church. Her and her husband were the youth pastors there. At that point in time I wasn't in a very healthy way; I felt stuck in a very unhealthy relationship.

I'll never forget that night, standing amongst what seemed like 1000 people while Pastor Steve Penny was preaching. I actually don't recall what he preached on, but at the end he simply asked, "If you would like prayer for something in your life then raise your hand and I'm going to pray for you." So I raised my hand, asking God to help. Nothing happened immediately, though I did not expect that to happen. But what did transpire over the next 10 months was nothing short of a miracle and was really a testament to God's grace and power.

Our holiday ended at the end of January and I returned to Townsville to start a Graduate Diploma in Clinical Exercise Physiology, I had just completed my bachelor's degree. To my surprise, the long relationship I had been in quickly ended. It was just shy of my 21st birthday and, for the first time in almost five years, I was single and really had no clue who I was.

One of my university placements was in Brisbane where my sister was living, and so I was able to stay with her during this time. To my amazement, my sister had just rededicated her life to Jesus. I was quite surprised to say the least, but was also curious as to what my sister was getting involved with. So, over the next three weeks, Lauren took me to a women's event which I actually loved. I went to her connect group which consisted of strong, intelligent, driven Christian girls, and to church. I had felt so uplifted that I knew on arriving home, I would need to find a church and get involved. I went to a couple churches, but they just didn't feel right. I would leave feeling condemned and knew they weren't right for me.

That year I was also representing James Cook University in netball at the University Games on the Gold Coast. During this time, I contracted glandular fever and, I'm pretty sure, was the sickest I have ever been in my entire life. Yet it made me realise again that I needed God in my life, and I definitely knew through this that I needed to get myself to church.

Finally, one of my dear friends from university invited me along to her church—Calvary Christian Church in Mt Louisa, Townsville. It was a 20-minute drive from where I was living, and I'll never forget the first time we tried to get there—finding ourselves lost and ending up at another smaller church we had come across on the drive home! Google maps on the iPhone didn't exist then.

At this point in time, I was working at the Mater Hospital in their Cardiac Rehabilitation Ward where I discovered one of the patients attended Calvary. On mentioning that we had actually tried to get there on the weekend prior, he kindly wrote me out a list of instructions, and I committed to try again the following Sunday night.

I don't really remember pulling up to church or walking in on my own that Sunday night, but I do remember walking through the auditorium doors. The church was full of life and there were so many young people my age. Initially I felt a little bit of anger—how could this place have existed 20 minutes from where I'd been living for the last four years and I had NO idea!

That Sunday night was the first Sunday night

that the former Senior Pastors took on the leadership of the church. I returned the following Sunday night, and at the end of the preach I rededicated my life to Jesus. It was October 4th, 2007. Three weeks later I was water baptized and was filled with the Holy Spirit immediately.

Shortly after that, my cousin and her husband, the ones who had invited me to church on Christmas Eve, moved to become the youth pastors of Calvary Christian Church in Townsville. So, I moved in and lived with them for the next 18 months or so. It really was the best unstructured discipleship program. At the start of the following year I became involved with the Red Frogs ministry at the University where I used to party—a lot! I now wanted to share the same love, grace and forgiveness that I had received. Over the next few years we saw many, many young adults come to know Jesus. I also got to witness my father giving his life to God.

Chapter 2

A WHOLE NEW WORLD

*Take delight in the Lord, and He will give you the
desires of your heart. (Psalm 37:4 NIV)*

I'll never forget the first time I saw Daniel. He was worship leading on stage, I was down the front in the Sunday night mosh pit at church and I remember looking up and seeing him and thinking, "Gee he's alright!"

I had been in church a few months (not long at all I know!) and I had heard from other girls how God can tell you who you are going to marry. So, I went home and let my request be known, ha! And I said to Jesus, "If Daniel is the one for me, then please make it obvious to me in the next seven days". I think back now to this prayer and laugh. Except, God did give me an answer.

On day three, I was out to coffee with a new friend from church and she told me how Daniel had just started dating. I think I was quite shocked at how quickly God did actually answer my prayer. So that was that then.

New young adult pastors had just started the Red Frog ministry (a university outreach ministry) at James Cook University. So, as I previously mentioned, I became very involved in this outreach which meant that every Thursday night I was handing out red frogs to university students at the University nightclub, all whilst working full time. Sunday mornings were spent voluntarily leading the café at church where we would prepare coffees for people who had just made a commitment to follow Jesus. Looking back, I am so grateful for this period of time when I was single and in church. It was such an exciting and refreshing season for me. I learnt how to trust God, and I remember realising that if I just kept running in my lane, at some point God would bring someone across my path who could run with me, even further and faster, together in the things that God had for us.

The following year I began Bible college, it was the first year of Calvary Leadership College. Not only would this be where and when I would be taught the Word of God, but I would also receive prophecies of the type of man I would marry—and of the anointing that is upon our lives. It changed my perspectives and Christian Worldview.

Halfway through my college year, I began getting accused of thinking that I was too good for all the guys. This was not the case at all, I just wasn't interested in any of them and didn't want to give the wrong impression that I was interested. In one morning-tea break we were having coffee out on the deck which oversaw the car park to the school where Daniel was working at the time as a School Chaplain. As we were sitting there, we noticed Daniel was walking across the car park towards the church. Sure enough, the person I was sitting beside asked me, "What about Daniel, what do you think about him? He's been single for a while now".

It wasn't too long after this that Daniel's brother and soon-to-be wife were getting married in Port Douglas. As I was quite close to them both because of serving in Red Frogs together, I was invited to their wedding. It was interesting because I had never really had a conversation with Daniel, but had many with his Mum when she volunteered on the church reception. I felt like I knew him from afar and that he was a part of an incredible family.

Anyway, back to the story... anyone who knows me, knows that I love to dance and that I'd never pass up an opportunity to do so. So here I was sitting at a table of mostly single young adults and wishing that I was dancing with Daniel! Life, or perhaps common sense, had taught me that there was no way Daniel was just going to walk over, interrupt a conversation with the whole table involved and ask me to dance. So instead, I got up and stood beside the dance floor by myself. Sure enough, the plan worked; he came over and asked me if I'd like to dance, and we did. It's kind of funny now thinking back, but it was worth it!

Of course, this got everybody at church talking about Daniel and Elise. A few days later I received a text from Daniel asking me out for a coffee. We went for coffee and I sat there rather confused as he proceeded to tell me that he wasn't dating anyone, that he just wanted to clarify that—not me, not anyone. I walked away and, to be honest, was also a little bit annoyed. I found out later that this was against his mother's better judgement. Apparently, she had told him not to invite me out to only let me know that he's not planning to date anyone.

A short while after, I was at a Hillsong conference and, during the part where they sell the pre-registrations for the following year's conference, I felt the Holy Spirit say to purchase two tickets—one ticket for me and one for Daniel. Yep, I'm that crazy person—and so I filled out two registrations, putting all of my contact details on them of course!

A few months passed and one afternoon, as I was sitting in my study studying for a Bible college exam, I felt led to pray. I wasn't sure what about, but knew I needed to. Sure enough, as I began to pray, the Holy Spirit showed me the anger and resentment that I was holding onto towards Daniel—all for simply rejecting me before we were even dating! As I prayed, the resentment lifted, and it was honestly like the Holy Spirit replaced it with a deep affection for him. I look back now and am so grateful for the leading of the Holy Spirit, but also rather grateful that I was obedient at that point in time. Things may have turned out rather differently had I held onto that bitterness I didn't even realise I felt.

At work the following week, I ran into one of my older patients. I was now working in a new job at James Cook University. She had no idea of my situation, however, she 'randomly' encouraged me with Psalm chapter 37, verse 4, 'Delight yourself in the Lord and He will give you the desires of your heart'. This was extremely 'random' because I didn't even know she was a Christian!

It wasn't long after this that the Bible college

PROMISE KEEPER

class of 2009 graduated. I had purchased a black gypsie dress with a gold trim and had my hair crimped. It was rather 'out there' for me—the hair that is. That night of graduation, I also received the bachelorette award and, as Dan was the master of ceremonies for the evening, he got to present me with the award. It's funny now thinking about it. Following the formal proceedings, we had, what I guess you would call, a Christian after-party where all night I could feel him staring at me! After this, I knew he was smitten.

My sister and cousin then decided to organise a New Year's Eve party, basically with the intention of getting us together. When the clock struck midnight, everyone went around in a circle hugging and cheering. When Daniel and I arrived face to face, Daniel gave me a wave and then kept going. It felt awkward and left me a little unsure of his feelings. Thankfully our friends intervened and followed up with him the next day asking if he had a case of the 'hot bum syndrome'. The 'hot bum syndrome' is described as a guy who really likes a girl but is too shy to talk to her or ask her out. Thank goodness Daniel accepted the reality of this condition and decided to be proactive as a result.

Within the first week of the New Year I was already back at work, and it was there where I received a text from Daniel asking me out for another coffee. I remember rocking up to coffee and Daniel had clearly been there for a little while. I didn't realise that I had originally sent him to the wrong coffee shop and that he had arrived there two hours earlier because he was so nervous.

After this, we went on a few coffee dates and he

told me that he didn't want to hold my hand or kiss me until he had asked my Dad if we could date. I was 23 years old and to that point in my life no one had ever asked my Dad if we could date, so it was rather special. I'll never forget Daniel coming over for dinner and then my Dad, Daniel and my mum going into the lounge room, clearly so that Daniel could ask my Dad. Daniel told me later it was like my Dad was a little shocked by Daniel asking him if he could date his daughter and didn't know what to say.

After a little while they came out, my mum was peaking and said, "I think Daniel has something to ask you". HAHA! Thankfully my Dad had agreed to us dating. Daniel and I then went out for a picnic where he asked me out. My response was, of course, yes!

The next 12 months were some of the most exciting and thrilling times. It was the start of a great new adventure and my favourite love story. Daniel honestly treated me like a princess, and I was totally in love.

On our very first Valentine's Day together he sent me flowers, picked me up and took me to breakfast and then dinner. He wrote me sweet letters, including sneaking 21 letters into my backpack when I went to Europe, just so that he could still make me smile every day I woke up, even though he wasn't with me. We laughed a lot, cried as we shared our previous hurts and disappointments, and dreamed of our future together. Everybody's story is different and ours was certainly not perfect, but I pray that every person has their own kind of love story. My prayer is that you don't ever give up believing that it either could happen for you, or that God would turn your current story around for good.

Chapter 3

THE PROPOSAL

*Now to him who is able to do immeasurably
more than all we ask or imagine, according to his
power that is at work within us.
(Ephesians 3:20 NIV)*

I always remember Daniel saying, that I would know a week out from when he was going to propose. Sure enough one Monday, we were meeting for coffee at the Coffee Club on the Strand. Cyclone Yasi has just passed through Townsville and many businesses were shut down or closed.

I'll never forget walking in to meet him and seeing the most beautiful large white glossy box wrapped in a white soft satin ribbon sitting on the coffee table in front of him. On top of the box was a gorgeous handwritten card which outlined that I was to be picked up on Saturday evening at 7pm sharp wearing what was in this beautiful large box! To my amazement, I opened the box to find the most stunning knee length, gold princess dress—a dress that I had actually tried on a month before when we were out shopping together. I had absolutely loved the dress but didn't end up purchasing it. Without my knowledge, he had returned later that afternoon to purchase the dress. How sweet!

Two days later we met again, which was a little out of the ordinary as we didn't often have a lot of time during the weeks to catch up. It was here that he gifted me with a beautiful picture of us in a gorgeous frame. On the frame, he had handwritten, "I love making fun-filled memories with you babe." It was very sweet! We then met up again on the Friday and he gave me yet another gift! However, this one threw me a little when I opened the gift box to find a pair of Havaianas (thongs). On the card, he asked me to bring these with a spare change of clothes on Saturday evening. To say I was a little excited was an understatement.

Of course, I was sharing all of this with my work colleagues as they were quite excited by it all. They also told me that if Daniel didn't propose, I'd be feeling pretty depressed come Monday. However, I felt quite sure it was going to happen. Daniel had always said it wouldn't be the greatest surprise *when* he was going to propose but the *way* in which he proposed would be. Well, he wasn't wrong.

We then met on Saturday for lunch, and I'll never forget how noticeably nervous Daniel was. I had never really seen Daniel nervous before, but he was on this day.

That evening, he arrived looking extremely handsome in a black suit and tie, holding the most beautiful bunch of long-stemmed red roses which were, and still are, my favourite. Mum got a quick photo of us and we were off. He had kindly borrowed one of our friend's cars which was really nice, and had even prearranged the music to suit the occasion. As we were driving, he turned to me and said that, as he was on his way over to pick me up, he had felt the Holy Spirit say to him, "This is the girl that you prayed for when you were 16".

This was a pretty big moment for me as I sat there driving along, my eyes tearing up thinking about where I was at all those years ago and what was going on in my life when he was praying for me. When I was 16 I didn't even know Daniel existed, we lived in completely different towns and at that point I wasn't in church regularly. If you had told me back then that this was going to, or could ever, happen I would have told you—maybe in a fairy-tale movie.

We had almost arrived at the restaurant, which was at a popular and prominent restaurant strip in Townsville, when we stopped at the crossing and watched as a few of our youth leaders, including my sister in law, walked across the road—with a three by two metre sign that read, "I love you Elise". It was super sweet and totally blew me away!

We then were at our favourite restaurant eating dinner, when the waiter approached our table holding his serving tray. As he got closer, I noticed a little white ring box on a tray. I gasped, thinking that this was the moment Daniel was going to propose. Only, when he opened the white ring box, two sea sickness tablets appeared. Daniel obviously knew from past experiences when he had taken me out on the water, that I got seasick. So, he asked me to take one now; I was definitely intrigued as to what was going on!

Shortly after dinner we left and went for dessert to a popular ice creamery on the waterfront. We arrived, and a friend of Daniel's was wearing a highly visible singlet (pretty sure it was borrowed from church) and ushered us into our carpark. I have no idea how long he had been standing there reserving the carpark for us. Apparently, someone had offered him $50 dollars just to park there! It was a popular spot for a Saturday night in Townsville.

As we were ordering dessert, I turned around and noticed many of our amazing family and friends sitting in the crowd. Again, I wondered if he was going to propose here in front of everyone (I had actually hoped not)! We sat down, right beside a band which was again filled with gifted musicians from church. Sure enough, there was a microphone stand there too and not long after we had started our dessert, Daniel jumped up and sang 'our song' to me—*You and I,* by Michael Bublé. I was speechless, Daniel had once again made me feel like an absolute princess.

By now I definitely felt like I was dreaming. As soon as he finished singing, he quickly swept me away and I waved goodbye to our friends and family. We jumped back in the car and he told me I could now put my thongs on. It was here that I knew this was it.

He pulled the car into the marina. We hopped out with my spare clothes and walked down the jetty where we could hear Michael Bublé music playing. Sure enough, Daniel had borrowed a friend's luxurious Riviera boat for the evening. Daniel mentioned to me that I could now get changed if I wished.

I had secretly wanted him to propose to me in

that dress so, instead of doing as Daniel had said, I went back to where he was. As I walked back, it was like Daniel quickly moved and asked if I had read the letter in the room? So, I went back to the room and there amongst some beautiful long-stemmed roses, I saw a letter. It was the most beautifully hand-written letter, and at the very end of the letter he signed off saying that he had a question to ask me and could I meet him on the back deck?

I walked back in my beautiful dress and there was Daniel, on one knee with the most beautiful ring I had ever seen (slightly bias of course). I can't even remember what he said but I definitely said YES!

He had literally thought of everything and had every detail planned. From purchasing mini sized Cokes (because he knows that's enough for me), to having my favourite chocolate on board. I was just absolutely smitten and so ready to spend the rest of my life with him. I'll never forget arriving home that night after he dropped me off, I literally felt like I was dreaming. You see, both of our Dads proposed to our Mums whilst driving along in a car. Fortunately for me, Daniel's mother had always said to him that he would need to make the way he proposed to Elise memorable. Well, he definitely achieved that! Four and a half months later we were married, and it was the second-best decision (other than Jesus) that I have ever made.

Jesus had been so kind to me. He had taken a pretty broken and insecure girl and gave me the desire of my heart. He had replaced negative words that had been previously spoken to me and over me, with His promises. He really did show me a whole new world, and I know He wants to do the same for you no matter what position or situation you are in.

...to bestow on them a crown of beauty instead of ashes, the oil of joy instead of mourning, and a garment of praise instead of a spirit of despair.
(Isaiah chapter 61, verse 3 NIV)

This is what Jesus wants to do for you and I according to His great power that is at work within us.
He loves us that much.

Chapter 4

THE DIAGNOSIS

I praise you because I am fearfully and wonderfully made; your works are wonderful, I know that full well. (Psalm 139:14 NIV)

*We walk by faith, not by sight.
(2 Corinthians 5:7 NIV)*

Throughout the season of Daniel and I dating, I would often end up in hospital with severe abdominal pain. If I was to describe it to you like I did with the doctors, I would liken it to the feeling of a knife scraping you on the inside—it was awful! It would also happen around the time of my period. The doctors in the emergency room would examine me and then send me for a scan, but they could never find anything. They'd suggested it may be a ruptured cyst, or it could be polycystic ovarian syndrome, but nothing definitive.

At this particular point in my life I was working as a clinical researcher for a Vascular Surgeon who also 'just happened' to work at the local private hospital. After probably frustrating my boss with requesting too much time off work and, of course, from his genuine care for my wellbeing, he took the liberty of referring me to one of his friends who 'just happened' to be one of the leading local gynaecologists.

Our first appointment with the gynaecologist went well and it was here that he requested I have a laparoscopy for further investigation. He said to me, "If you wake up after surgery and see just one incision bandaged, you'll know I didn't find anything. If you wake up after surgery with two or more, you'll know I found something."

I woke up and saw three bandaged incisions! Not long after this, our gynaecologist came to see me and told me, "It will be very difficult for you to have children due to the location and the amount of the endometriosis we found. We have removed it all, but I will prescribe you a particular type of the pill that will help keep it at bay."

It was December of 2010; Daniel and I had been dating for almost 12 months and were getting married the following June. I had never heard of Endometriosis let alone realised that I had this condition. At least now I could finally understand where the pain was originating. Endometriosis Australia[1] describes Endometriosis as being present when the tissue that is similar to the lining of the uterus (womb) occurs outside this layer and causes pain and/or infertility. The lining layer is called the endometrium, and this is the layer of tissue that is shed each month with menstruation (period) or where a pregnancy grows and settles.

The annoying thing with Endometriosis is that it can, and often does, grow back even after ablation/

surgical removal.

Up until this point I hadn't had a strong desire for children. I knew one day I would have a family, but I was always more focused on my career and setting myself up financially. I was also working at a university where I was influenced by strong opinions; maternity leave was classified as a career disruption, or at least that was how you referred to it in your resume. It's amazing how much you don't realise you want something until you are told that you can't have it.

That evening I went home pretty drugged up on morphine and feeling pretty low.

God often speaks to me in dreams. It's almost like He wakes me up sometimes to show me something or speak to me about something. That night God gave me a picture of Daniel holding a little boy, our son. It was amazing, and a promise from God that I would hold onto.

Over the next couple of years, Daniel began to minister in some of the churches in the surrounding areas. He would also share our story of the diagnosis that had been given to us and the promise from God that we were standing on—that he would give us a son. In September of 2013 we decided to go off the pill, and a week later Daniel went back to minister at the same church where he had shared our story 12 months prior. After he had finished speaking, a more mature woman came up to him and said, "Since you came 12 months ago, I have been praying for you and your wife that you would conceive, and right now I'd like to pray a blessing over you that you would take home to your wife." Well, Daniel arrived home and a couple weeks later I did a pregnancy test, as I had been having terrible back pain. To our absolute amazement we were pregnant! I honestly could not believe it. How good is God!

We had only just found out that we were pregnant when my sister-in-law told me that she too was expecting! I thought at the time that we must be pretty close. But we didn't want to announce our pregnancy just yet, as we also wanted to celebrate firstly with them. Daniel and I had already decided that we wanted to wait and tell everyone together. It was funny because it was probably six months before this when a couple had told us a similar story of how this happened to them. One couple had just found out but hadn't told anyone, then their closest friends had told them that they were expecting too.

We had planned to wait for the seven-week dating scan and a photo of course, before we told our family. So, a couple days after we had this booked in, we organised for a big family dinner. We had made up a story saying that the dinner was to thank both sets of parents as we had lived with them whilst building our house. Then, just before we started eating, we handed both sets of parents a 'thank you card' which included the seven-week ultrasound scan. Their different responses were hilarious. My in-laws were the first ones to open the card. My sister, who was sitting beside them who saw the ultrasound scan (and clearly knew what it was), ripped it out of my in-law's hands, stood up and screamed. My father then stood up and yelped. Later we found out that he thought we had sent him and Mum on an overseas holiday! Sorry Dad, not this time.

Then on the 24th June 2014, our son, Jonathan (name meaning 'Gift from God') David Daniel Pappas was born and exactly a week following, my niece Jaya Milan Pappas was welcomed into the world.

You see, in that time-period of two years and eight months between the diagnosis and finding out that we were indeed pregnant, I had to keep replacing the words that our specialist had given me with the vision God had granted me of our son. After every appointment we had with our specialist, who would encourage us to hurry up and start trying straight away (before we were even married mind you!), I would have to replace that with the vision and promise God gave me. Every single time, over and over again.

We walk by faith and not by sight, so instead of believing the diagnosis someone gave you and the words that others have spoken over your life, ask God for a heavenly promise, a Scripture to replace that thought or fear with. This didn't mean I didn't keep seeking wisdom and advice from our specialist or that I didn't go on a pill to help keep the Endometriosis at bay. We certainly did everything we could and were advised to do in the natural until we decided to start 'trying'. Sometimes we think that walking by faith and not by sight means not doing much of anything, and expecting God to do everything. But the key word in this is 'walk', and that as we walk—verb, it's a *doing* word, that He will do everything He can too.

I continued to speak out that I was fearfully and wonderfully made. His Word is true.

John chapter 1, verse 14 (NIV) says:

The Word became flesh and made his dwelling among

us. We have seen his glory, the glory of the one and only Son, who came from the Father, full of grace and truth.

People may tell us what they believe to be true. But it is the Word of God that is absolute truth, and Scripture promises that it doesn't return empty but accomplishes the purpose with which He sent it!

> ...so is my word that goes out from my mouth: It will not return to me empty, but will accomplish what I desire and achieve the purpose for which I sent it. (Isaiah chapter 55, verse 11 NIV)

What promises has God spoken over your life that you need reminding of today? Keep believing! Keep declaring! He has not forgotten you.

Chapter 5

ARABELLA

Italian name meaning – A beautiful altar/sacrifice[2]
Latin name meaning – Yielding to prayer[3]

Now that we were in the season of having kids, I loved the idea of having a little girl. I mean, how adorable it would be to see Daniel holding a little girl in his arms. The interesting thing, however, was that when I was pregnant with our son Jonathan, and at the time unsure of the sex, I really felt like God had given me the name Arabella. Arabella means a 'beautiful sacrifice'. The meaning of the name puzzled me as I really felt strongly that it was from God, so I incorrectly assumed that I must be pregnant with a girl. I later realised that Arabella was a promise to come.

In January 2015, we relocated to the Sunshine Coast to become the Youth Pastors at the Sunshine Coast Campus. We had only just moved into our brand-new home six months earlier, but knew this move was of God. Then in April 2015, shortly after we had moved into a three-bedroom townhouse in Buderim, I was going about my day at home with our son when I walked into our bedroom and God gave me a vision of a little girl standing there right in front of me. At the same time, Daniel and I had been talking about trying again, we had even begun speaking about girl names and we both agreed that we liked the name Sophie. So almost straight after, we decided to try again. Little did I realise the significance of this vision and the journey that we were about to embark on. Shortly before Jonathan's first birthday, which was at the end of June, we found out that we were pregnant—we were ecstatic at how quickly we had fallen pregnant again! So, as we were celebrating Jonathan's first birthday, we began to tell people that we were expecting baby number two.

Two weeks following, we were holding our annual youth camp. We were somewhere a little remote, so we had little phone reception and it was here that I began feeling unwell. Daniel was very kind and agreed I should go back to our room for some of the camp. I didn't realise it at the time, but it was here that I began to experience signs of a miscarriage. We arrived home and Daniel left straight away to fly to Townsville to attend the North Youth Camp held in Mission Beach. The next time I spoke to him was at 4am the following morning after I had woken up in awful pain and was experiencing loss. While we had been looking after other people's children, we were losing our own.

I was devastated, and after a few sleepless hours I opened my Bible to Psalm chapter 27, verse 13:

> I remain confident of this: I will see the goodness of
> the LORD in the land of the living.

PROMISE KEEPER

Here was a promise from Heaven, that I would see the goodness of God in the land of the living. How truly kind He is!

Thankfully, a friend who didn't even live locally, 'randomly' text me that morning and asked if I had time to grab a coffee. I replied asking her, instead of coffee, could she take me to the doctor? That day was spent driving from the doctor's surgery to ultrasound, to blood test, back to the doctor which confirmed my greatest fear—that I was no longer pregnant. My friend then drove me up to the hospital that night where I would get my first Anti D injection; an injection that was necessary at the time due to Daniel's blood group being positive and mine being negative. I remember sitting at the coffee shop with my friend over lunch that day with our son Jonathan. We didn't speak all that much, but her company meant more to me than 1000 words. I wasn't familiar with the term 'miscarriage'; it wasn't something that was known by my mum or that I had ever spoken about. I was quite early on—just shy of seven weeks pregnant, and had many questions surrounding it. Like, was it an actual baby?

We decided to wait a few months before trying again and then in October of 2015, we found out we were pregnant again, praise God! I was a little worried if what had happened before would happen again, but we were hopeful and faith-filled. After having some time away, we excitedly went to see our doctor, but when we mentioned that we were pregnant, his expression was anything but excited. He was cautious and that was fair enough, so off we went for more blood tests to see how the pregnancy was progressing and I was advised to rest. We were advised to have another appointment with him the following week however, the following day, on the Saturday morning when I was getting ready to go out for coffee, Daniel came in saying that we needed to see the doctor straight away. You see, Daniel had gone downstairs and had noticed the numbers of missed calls on both of our phones from the medical centre. My heart sank, this wasn't good.

I went in to see the doctor who said it was extremely likely that I was going to have yet another miscarriage, my HCG reading was very low (Beta human chorionic gonadotropin (HCG) is a hormone produced by the placenta during pregnancy, and is typically detected in the blood[4]). He sent me off to pick up some medication in an attempt to help keep our baby alive. We hadn't even told any of our family that we were pregnant yet but now instead, we asked them to believe with us for a miracle. But God had other plans for this little child and within hours I experienced our second miscarriage.

We were devastated—I hadn't known pain like this before. But what I was about to realise is that I also hadn't known my God like this before either. To have one miscarriage is heart-breaking. Statistics say that one in four women miscarry[5]. But to have two miscarriages and within three months? That apparently only happens to 2% of the population[6]. And unfortunately, until you have had three, which is then termed as recurrent miscarriages[7]— no one is required to do any further investigation.

At this point in time, my parents had been caravanning around Australia, but that afternoon they just happened to arrive on our doorstop. To have my husband, parents and family with us was extremely comforting. And even though we were experiencing such heartache I could sense His wrap-around presence (Psalm chapter 84, verse 9, TPT).

I knew I needed a little extra help to get through this, so I contacted our church's Counsellor who was a dear old pastor. I struggled with questions surrounding the losses of life. I always appreciated my time with the Counsellor as we would pray through the different things. So, on this particular day we asked Jesus to give me a vision of how He saw these two children.

God gave me the most magical vision. It was a vision of them, they were slightly older, and they were kneeling before God, who was this almighty light that shone. I knew then that our children were indeed in heaven, spending eternity with Jesus. This meant that I could release them to Jesus there and then. I also learnt that I could ask Jesus to pass messages on to our children. Something I still do today.

The following twelve months were a little tricky, celebrating with Jonathan as he got older but also processing the pain that we had experienced, all whilst searching for answers and still trying to fall pregnant.

Then Easter of 2016 rolled around and one of our good friends gave me a prophecy that she had had a picture of Daniel and I being interviewed on stage with a little girl sitting on our lap and her name meant wisdom. A few days later I went down to the park where I would regularly take Jonathan and there was a child's hat upside down which had SOPHIE in whiteout written along the underside of the brim. Maybe it was just a coincidence, but I looked up the meaning of the name 'Sophie' and sure enough its meaning was 'wisdom'. That was pretty amazing and a massive injection of faith for me.

But then, in October of 2016, I was on my way out of the house to our church's weekly women's get together when I thought I would take a pregnancy test—sure enough two lines appeared, I was pregnant! We went to the doctor straight after the meeting and, of course, I was sent for more blood tests straight away. However, unfortunately before I even had blood drawn, I started miscarrying. This was now our third miscarriage.

That night I was so sad, just so sad and frustrated. Why did this keep happening? I was doing everything I could in the natural. By this stage I had seen a natural hormone therapist, numbers of doctors, we had prayed numbers of times, we had been prayed for countless times. I began to dislike my body for not doing what it should just be able to do.

Daniel was so kind throughout it all, but that night I just needed to go for a drive alone. I drove down to the beach and parked along the front, right in front of the beach. As I sat there, I looked at two big old trees that stood between the beach and where I had parked. One looked so withered and worn, you could see its root system was pretty much non-existent. The other tree stood firm and strong, its root system was clearly strong—there were many thick roots. In that moment I felt the Holy Spirit ask me, "Which one do you want to be? Do you want to be like the tree that withstands the test of time and the many different seasons that life will throw your way? Or do you want to be like the other tree that looks withered and weary?" I decided I wanted my life to be like the strong tree, and knew that in order to do this, I needed to strengthen my relationship with Jesus.

PROMISE KEEPER

At the same time, I was growing the most beautiful petunias in our garden. We didn't get the opportunity to bury our other little ones as it was so early on. But this child was a little older so when they passed, Daniel and I decided that we would bury our little one amongst our pretty petunias. It was so surreal and to this day, still seems that way. But we stood there that night and prayed, and again released our little one Heaven's way. I believe God has a special place in heaven for all the little ones.

Not long after this, I decided by faith to buy a name sign that read 'Sophie', believing that one day we would hang it above her cot in her room. We prayed over it and stood in faith that one day soon I would become pregnant with our Sophie girl.

In August of 2017 we were delighted to find out that we were pregnant. Naturally I was a little fearful, but we were expectant that God would deliver on His promise. Unfortunately, within a few weeks I began to miscarry again. My tummy had blown up and I was in a lot of pain. I had fought and prayed for this little miracle and I was not ready to give him or her over to Jesus. I couldn't believe I was miscarrying again. In that moment, I felt the Holy Spirit speak to me: "Elise just hand her over," and I knew it was our little Arabella, our beautiful sacrifice.

Recently we attended a memorial service for our friend's beautiful daughter, Arabella. She had passed away whilst in utero and as I sat there and listened to the words spoken over her life by the Pastor, it brought me much healing regarding our Arabella. He said, "It seems that God had made Arabella all for himself." You see,

I had written out dreams for our Arabella, but now my eyes had been open to perhaps her real purpose in life.

Chapter 6

PURPOSE IN YOUR PAIN

... fixing our eyes on Jesus, the pioneer and perfecter of faith. For the joy set before him he endured the cross, scorning its shame, and sat down at the right hand of the throne of God.
(Hebrews 12:2 NIV)

A life of faith isn't absent of pain or loss. Jesus knew pain.

Think about the cat of nine tails and the scorning that Jesus received (1 Kings chapter 12, verses 11). It was excruciating, agonizing and traumatizing—not exactly what you would call pain free!

If, like me, you too believe that Jesus is both God and human, then every feeling we feel, it too has been felt by Him. To think that Jesus doesn't understand our pain is just plain wrong. Unfortunately, many walk away from their faith when facing a difficulty. But Jesus didn't make that bad thing happen, he actually understands the pain that we are facing. When we grasp a hold of this fact, that He endured the cross for our sake, we certainly should not blame Him for what we are going through but rather be grateful for what He went through.

How could we say that Jesus doesn't care or that He doesn't love us?

We were recently saddened by some news surrounding a couple of our friends. We didn't know what else to do, so we prayed. In that moment, I had a picture of Jesus leaning over, arms around us grieving also.

No matter what we feel, He has felt it too—the anger, the heartache, the loss, the utter frustration, the devastation, the agony.

After we had our fourth miscarriage, I knew I needed help to process all that had gone on. I hadn't realised the blame that I had attached to God. Without even realising it, I had felt that God had made me go through all of this. What I came to learn was that what He promises is seed, time and harvest but He can't always guarantee the outcome. We live in a sinful world and have each been given free will—choice. This was a major breakthrough for me and one that I didn't even know that I needed. It was not God's fault that my body was rejecting these pregnancies. God, like any loving father, would have loved nothing more than to protect me from such pain or whatever was going on.

In that moment I became free and felt like I could go on and move forward again in my relationship with Jesus. He is a loving God who is on our side!

Jesus was able to endure the cross because of the joy set before him. The joy of our eternities being forever changed, the joy of Him being seated at the right hand of God.

> The fact that our heart yearns for something Earth can't supply is proof that Heaven must be our Home. (C.S Lewis)

Shortly after my husband became a Christian, he had a vision—it was like a movie trailer. The movie trailer was of Jesus being scourged, and after every scourging that Jesus received, Jesus would yell, "It was all for you Daniel!" Jesus went to the cross for the whole world, but He also went to the cross for you and I. The pain that we've felt, He identifies with it and He empathises with us.

Job chapter 1 verses 6-12 (NIV):

> One day the angels came to present themselves before the Lord, and Satan also came with them. The Lord said to Satan, "Where have you come from?"
> Satan answered the Lord, "From roaming throughout the earth, going back and forth on it." Then the Lord said to Satan, "Have you considered my servant Job? there is no one on earth like him; he is blameless and upright, a man who fears God and shuns evil."
> "Does Job fear God for nothing?" Satan replied. "Have you not put a hedge around him and his household and everything he has? You have blessed the work of his hands, so that his flocks and herds are spread throughout the land. But now stretch out your hand and strike everything he has, and he will surely curse you to your face."

> The Lord said to Satan, "Very well, then, everything he has is in your power, but on the man himself do not lay a finger."
> Then Satan went out from the presence of the Lord.

Job chapter 2 verses 7-10 (NIV):

> So, Satan went out from the presence of the Lord and afflicted Job with painful sores from the soles of his feet to the crown of his head. Then Job took a piece of broken pottery and scraped himself with it as he sat among the ashes.
> His wife said to him, "Are you still maintaining your integrity? Curse God and die!"
> He replied, "You are talking like a foolish woman. Shall we accept good from God, and not trouble?"
> In all this, Job did not sin in what he said.

Despite what Job had been through, the hardships he faced and what he lost, he doesn't curse God. And so as in Job chapter 42 verse 10, we see God returning to Job twice as much as he had before. This is a great promise for us when going through and handling our pain—cling to Jesus, and no matter what is taken away He will always return double.

God will never give us more than we can handle, we can be sure of that.

It's also good to remember that there will always be purpose in our pain. We may not realise it at the time, but we will in the future. Perhaps it will give us empathy for others going through similar circumstances or wisdom in knowing how to handle different situations.

PROMISE KEEPER

There is always a purpose to it.

The first time I had to go to the hospital after I miscarried, my cousin, who is a nurse, came with me. At the hospital where my cousin worked, women who experienced a miscarriage received a little pack to take home with them. It included a handmade bag with a magnet which had some comforting words on it, and some information with a number to contact for further support. It was a lovely, thoughtful gift, and they handed them out because women would come in pregnant, though miscarrying, and leave without a baby or being pregnant any longer.

The hospital that I was at didn't have anything like this. So, after the second miscarriage and experiencing the same thing with the hospital, I spoke to my friend and our church's women's team to see if this was something we could action. We decided to raise money to purchase a number of Chris Pringle's book, *Jesse*. It is a beautiful book where Chris writes about their son whom she miscarried and who is now in heaven. We put a sticker on the front of the books to let women and families know this gift was from the women at our church, and gave them to the chaplain at the hospital.

Just like there was purpose to Jesus' pain, there is always purpose to our pain too.

Chapter 7

FRUIT IN THE DESERT

By their fruit you will recognize them. Do people pick grapes from thorn bushes, or figs from thistles? Likewise, every good tree bears good fruit, but a bad tree bears bad fruit. A good tree cannot bear bad fruit, and a bad tree cannot bear good fruit. Every tree that does not bear good fruit is cut down and thrown into the fire. Thus, by their fruit you will recognize them. (Matthew 7:16-20 NIV)

There were times throughout this stage in our life where life felt a little dry, personally. In other areas of our lives, things were going great, but our personal life felt like a bit like a desert. It was at these times someone would 'randomly' offer to look after Jonathan, bring me a gift, or clean our house and honestly, these acts of kindness were like being given fresh, juicy pieces of fruit to eat along the way.

The Bible refers to literal fruit—such as olives, grapes and figs—many times. But more frequently, the Bible uses the word 'fruit' in a symbolic sense. Jesus did this when he said that our lives should bare good fruit in Matthew chapter seven.

God's desire for us is to produce good fruit and to produce a lot of it. Jesus said:

> This is to my Father's glory, that you bear much fruit,
> showing yourselves to be my disciples.
> (John chapter 15, verse 8 NIV).

Notice that bearing abundant fruit glorifies God and identifies Christ's disciples! Later, Jesus states the purpose of our calling: "You did not choose me, but I chose you and appointed you to go and bear fruit—fruit that will last" (John chapter 15, verse 16 NIV). Hence, we must be oriented toward eternal goals and work with all our hearts to bring them to fruition!

We are commanded to bear fruit. As believers, **our lives should be marked by bearing fruit**. It is one thing to profess faith in Jesus. But it is another thing to produce the fruit—the evidence of faith in Jesus.

We often think that when the conditions are perfect we will bear fruit. But God's desire for us to bear fruit is not determined by whether the conditions or seasons are perfect. We are called to bear fruit in and out of season. This isn't always easy, especially when faced with a difficult season or challenging circumstances. So how do we do it? How do we bear fruit in the desert?

You bear fruit in the desert when you remain connected to the vine.

Jesus says in John chapter 15, verse 4 (NIV):

PROMISE KEEPER

Remain in me, as I also remain in you. No branch can bear fruit to itself; it must remain in the vine. Neither can you bear fruit by itself; it must remain in the vine. Neither can you bear fruit unless you remain in me.

We bear fruit when we remain connected to Jesus.

I distinctly remember driving to church after the second miscarriage and I heard that quiet, still voice ask me, "If you weren't a pastor Elise, would you still be going to church?" That day is so etched in my memory. I came home from church and made a very deliberate decision that I was going to dig in deep in my relationship with God. I became even more intentional in spending time with Jesus.

Why? Because one day I wanted to exit this current season with my relationship with Jesus still intact.

When the branch is connected to the vine it can seem to the branch like not much is happening. But that is because the branch cannot see what the vine is doing under the ground.

When we were building our first home, it seemed to take a rather long time to get to the stage where the walls were going up. So much had to happen at a foundational level first. Anyone who has ever built anything knows that the foundation and framework are the most important part of the build. You can't really see the fruit to begin with, just the disruption and annoyance it has caused—but soon you'll be able to.

Sometimes we experience situations and circumstances and they allow us to decide: will we trust Jesus and choose to go deeper in our relationship?

The story of Job from the Bible may help us to better understand this concept. He is a man who God declared was upright and blameless in His sight. Satan comes along and, in summary, says: "But what about when you stop blessing him, and take away all that he has?"

So, God allows it. A lot of awful things take place; his own sons and daughters die, his wife encourages him to curse God. However, Job held to his convictions and, although he may have questioned God, he still trusted in God, chose to worship God and recognised that God was his Saviour. And so, it says in the Bible that God gave back to Job twice as much as he had before:

> The Lord blessed the latter part of Job's life more than the former part. He had fourteen thousand sheep, six thousand camels, a thousand yoke of oxen and a thousand donkeys. And he also had seven sons and three daughters... After this, Job lived a hundred and forty years... (Job chapter 42 verses 12-13,16 NIV)

We produce, not just profess, God's goodness in our lives by remaining connected to the vine.

There is fruit in the desert when you have a confident expectation of fruit

Hope is a positive expectation of good.
It creates an environment of confident expectation.

> For we were saved in this hope, but hope that is seen is not hope; for why does one still hope for what

he sees? But if we hope for what we do not see, we eagerly wait for it with perseverance.
(Romans chapter 8, verses 24-25 NKJV)

A little while ago we decided it would be nice to be able to grow our own tomatoes. We dried some seeds and planted them in the ground, and do you know what happened? Nothing—for about two weeks. Then there were little stalks which didn't look very promising. But we had an expectation of fruit, and today our tomato bushes are fruit producing machines!

At any point, we could have said that these plants didn't look like they were ever going to produce fruit, and ripped them out. But we had a confident expectation and so we waited.

David writes in Psalm 12 verse 6 (TPT):

His truth is tested, found to be flawless and ever faithful. It's as pure as silver refined seven times in a crucible of clay.

We had a promise from God for future children and so our hope was, and is, in Him and His word, not in circumstance. Circumstances change but He promises that His word will not return void (Isaiah chapter 55, verses 11 NLT).

We ought to be prisoners of hope (Zechariah chapter 9, verses 12 NIV)—people that carry hope everywhere we go, who encourage others to hope in the same way. Hope helps us walk out difficult and tricky seasons well.

David writes in Psalm chapter 42 verse 11, that hope helps our countenance: "for I shall praise Him, the help of my countenance and my God."

I once heard someone say that a person who keeps smiling at Jesus through the good and the bad, is pretty remarkable. But this is possible when we have hope.

And although we may feel we are like a broken vessel, as the Psalmist writes, we must remember that this broken vessel is in the hands of a divine potter. What a powerful thing that is!

God wants us to create environments of confident expectation. We are His children who wait expectantly for good things to happen! Wait expectantly for fruit in our lives. We realise that it may take time, but we don't quit, we don't give up!

Hebrews chapter 6, verses 18-19 (MSG):

> We who have run for our very lives to God have every reason to grab the promised hope with both hands and never let go.

There's fruit in the desert when we have a confident expectation of fruit!

There's fruit in the desert when you allow the fruit to ripen.

Fruit takes time to grow, to develop, to sweeten. It doesn't happen overnight! Sometimes we grow impatient, weary and we pick the fruit too early—it tastes foul and it's unpleasant! But don't get frustrated, don't grow weary.

PROMISE KEEPER

Keep on believing!

Abraham waited 25 years for his promise to be fulfilled. Abraham and Sarah could have settled with Ishmael, but they knew there was something more. Sometimes you and I just have to wait a little longer for our promise to come to pass!

David spent a great deal of his time waiting. David had to wait something like 15 years from the time he was first anointed by Samuel to the time he became king over Israel.

Joseph went from a pit, to a prison cell, to a palace. He patiently waited for God's promises to come about.

When we wait and allow the fruit to ripen, it produces something greater within us! It develops our character, and endurance, and it shapes us.

If the enemy cannot stop you from producing fruit then he will try to convince you to pick it too early.

There were times in our journey when I would rush ahead of God and try to do it in our own strength, rather than realising God wanted to do more in us first. There were certainly times when I would get frustrated with the process and the simple fact that I wasn't getting any younger. Yet God had the perfect timing.

Isaiah chapter 43, verses 19 (NIV):

> See, I am doing a new thing! Now it springs up; do you not perceive it? I am making a way in the wilderness and streams in the wasteland.

In the book of Ezekiel, chapter 47, we see Jerusalem being burned, 700 people leaving, and they all felt like God was against them. But Ezekiel serves these 700 people, he holds onto God and God gives him a dream of rebuilding God's Temple.

Ezekiel chapter 47, verses 1 and 12 (NLT):

> In my vision, the man brought me back to the entrance of the Temple. There I saw a stream flowing east from beneath the door of the Temple and passing to the right of the altar on its south side. (verse 1)

> Fruit trees of all kinds will grow along both sides of the river. The leaves of these trees will never turn brown and fall, and there will always be fruit on their branches. There will be a new crop every month, for they are watered by the river flowing from the Temple. The fruit will be for food and the leaves for healing. (verse 12)

In summary: every month they will bear fruit and there will always be fruit on their branches.

God promises that there will be fruit in the desert. Whenever we talk about the desert, it's the place we're trying to avoid. No one in their right mind embraces the desert because we all want easier lives, we all would naturally prefer to live comfortably. However, God wants sweeter fruit.

God's ultimate goal is NOT for our comfort but for HIS glory.

PROMISE KEEPER

A brilliant quote by Kristian Paul Anderson reads:

> There is a crack in everyone, that's how the light gets in... It's the light that permeates the brokenness. It's the light that the three wise men followed that night when Christ was born. It's the light that just came to be when God said: "let there be light" on the first day of creation. It's unexplainable.

I think most would like to be living as if we were on a permanent holiday, avoiding the difficulties and stresses of life, yet we should embrace the desert. It's in the desert that you and I bear the sweetest fruit because at the end of the day—this is what life is all about—the pursuit of the sweetest grace. When I look back now at that time in our lives when we experienced such loss and pain, it's like I almost grieve how close I felt to Jesus.

A quote from the Matthew Henry Commentary, on Ezekiel chapter 47 reads:

> That the reason of this extraordinary fruitfulness is, because their waters (talking about root system) issued out of the sanctuary; it is not ascribed to anything but to the continual supplies of Divine Grace with which they are watered every moment, that gave the increase.

I hope as you read this, you'll be encouraged in the things that you are believing for, that you will not stagger in the promises that He has given you, but rather you'll have greater assurance of them. That despite your circumstances you will continue to believe for greater fruit.

Chapter 8

PERSEVERANCE

Therefore, since we are surrounded by such a great cloud of witnesses, let us throw off everything that hinders and the sin that so easily entangles. And let us run with perseverance the race marked out for us, fixing our eyes on Jesus, the pioneer and perfecter of faith. (Hebrews 12:1-2 NIV)

The very definition of the word 'perseverance' means: ***to persist in doing something despite difficulty or delay in achieving success.*** [8]

In year 12, I completed the Duke of Edinburgh Gold Expedition. My classmates and I were to complete the Thorsborne Trail on Hinchinbrook Island in North Queensland, Australia, hiking from the southern point to the northern point of the island. We had everything we would need for the 32 kilometre walk which we were due to complete over a three night, four-day expedition.

What we had not anticipated was a sudden change in weather as we started our expedition. Torrential rain bucketed down, as only it can in the tropical north. By the time we had made it to the halfway point, Zoe Bay, we had already trekked through chest-deep water and had limited dry clothing left. On the third day, as we left camp at Zoe Bay to continue our trek north, we were stopped before the first river. The current was far too strong and dangerous with large debris rushing past. I'll never forget the moment that we stood there on the rocks at the edge of the river with our hike leaders investigating whether we could cross it. But it just wasn't going to be possible.

How often does life produce these moments—where we find ourselves standing at the edge of a seemingly impossible situation?

Here we were, stranded on the island between the overflowing river on the north side and now the overflowing river on the south side. The only food I had left by this point were two Nutella hazelnut spread packets and a muesli bar.

On the third night as my friend and I were going to bed, we could hear something in our tent, so I sat up and had a bit of a look around. I then felt a four-legged creature run up my spine! We had a rat in our tent and that rat had just crawled up my back! My friend and I ran out of the tent screaming. Sure enough we woke up everyone in our friend's tent that was right near ours. They began screaming. One of the guys even ran out of his tent, tripped over the tent peg and fell face first onto the ground. We were tired, wet, hungry and frightened. Needless to say, I could not wait to get off the island.

Each morning and afternoon, our teacher would walk two kilometres up the beach in the rain to get signal so he could try and call back to the mainland to sort how we were going to get off the island. By doing this he was able to get a greater perspective. Upon his return each morning and afternoon he would update us of the situation, the current weather and water conditions, and inform us of the likelihood of when we may be able to get off the island. Thankfully on day four in the late afternoon, we received wonderful news that we should be able to hike back to the southern point the following morning (day five) to catch the boat back to the mainland. If we weren't going to be able to hike, then we would be helicoptered off. By this stage we were now making headlines across the state news.

Due to the weather and sea forecasts that morning, we had to hike in one morning what took us two and a half days previously. We were literally running in wet clothes, with backpacks that weighed a lot more because they were drenched. Thankfully we made it to the boat on time and were safely taken back to the mainland. Never have I been more excited to see my parents and to eventually arrive home and sleep in my own bed!

The expedition may not have gone to plan but that's the nature of expeditions. You never really know what adventure lays ahead until you take the first brave step.

Life is a lot like this. So often we start off with a dream in our heart, only to hit a few roadblocks, detours and flooded rivers along the way.

There were many times when believing for another child, I would ask Daniel if I was crazy to believe for this? Mainly because everything that happened in the natural seemed so contrary to what God said and what the Bible promises. Even well-meaning family and friends encouraged us, after all we had been through, to perhaps just stop trying and be content with what we had.

Yet we carried a promise in our heart and a word from God and because of that I just couldn't, as much as it would have probably been easier to, give up. We decided that even if it tarries, we will wait for it! David writes in Psalm chapter 27, verses 13-14 (AMPC):

> What would have become of me had I not believed that I would see the Lord's goodness in the land of the living. Wait, hope for and expect the Lord. Be brave and of good courage. Let your heart be stout and enduring. You won't be put to shame.

The Scripture encourages us that the posture of our heart matters, especially when persevering.

Hebrews chapter 6, verse 12 (NIV):

> We do not want you to become lazy, but to imitate those who through faith and patience inherit what has been promised.

Sometimes persevering looks like imitating others who, by keeping their faith and remaining patient, inherited what has been promised.

Most of us are probably okay with the first one mentioned—faith, because it is a common mark of a believer. But what about patience? Especially when we live in a world where many things happen in a moment! Patience, as described by the Cambridge Dictionary,[9] is the capacity to accept or tolerate delay, problems, or suffering without becoming annoyed or anxious.

Easier said than done! Yet the reward is, by imitating others with faith and patience, we will inherit the promises of God.

Don't quit, don't give up, give it one more try. Perspective also helps when persevering. God's perspective, His point of view, matters and is the most important.

David wrote in Psalm chapter 12, verse 6-7 (AMP):

> The words and promises of the Lord are pure words, like silver refined in an earthen furnace, purified seven times over.
> You will keep them and preserve them. You will guard and keep us from evil.

David compares His word to silver being refined in an earthly vessel, seven times over. In our own humanity we may become discouraged, but His promises never fade. He will keep them and preserve them.

We must believe in the integrity of God's Word:
That He is who He says He is
That He'll do what He says He can do

If we want to see God's power outworked in our lives, then we must move forward according to the finished work on the cross, NOT our natural feelings, emotions or circumstances.

Don't give up! Keep on persisting!

In the book of Esther, we see a woman who doesn't give up, who keeps on persisting, and so she finds favour in the eyes of the King. What reward lies on the other side of your perseverance?

Augustine, a theologian and philosopher who was hugely influential in the development of Western Christianity wrote:

> ...that no one can be sure of salvation in this life, that man may have grace now but unless **God grants the gift of perseverance man will not maintain it to the end.**

Let me encourage you to be a person of perseverance, like a dog to a bone. Keep at it! Keep working, keep trying new things, you just never know how near you are to receiving that breakthrough and inheriting that promise!

Keep preserving till the end! Don't give up!
You will succeed! You will conquer!
You will breakthrough in Jesus name.

Chapter 9

HOLDING PATTERN

*So cheer up! Take courage all you who love Him.
Wait for Him to breakthrough for you, all who trust
in Him. (Psalm 31:24 TPT)*

A holding pattern is the name given to a flight path maintained by an aircraft awaiting permission to land[10]. It is a state of waiting or suspended activity of progress. It happens to planes even in regional airports, where pilots ready to land are asked to complete a left or right orbit or multiple until they are informed that the airway is clear. It can happen randomly and, as a pilot, you don't always expect it or 'are able to' anticipate it.

For example, the pilot of a smaller plane can be asked to hold because, although unseen, there is a much bigger plane flying in from a long way off at a much faster speed. Holding patterns can also happen at places you wouldn't expect them to—they don't only happen near the airport. The flight controllers, who are the ones in control of such things, contact the pilot and explain what to do. It is a process, and though the plane isn't really going anywhere other than going around in circles, the process is in place so that the path ahead can be cleared. All the pilot can do is hold, be patient and wait.

We all have seasons in our lives where we are waiting: waiting on something, waiting for that next job to come along, waiting for a promotion or pay rise, waiting for a special someone, waiting for a baby. Apparently the greatest disappointment in life is unmet expectations. For example—when I thought something would happen but then the opposite or perhaps nothing at all happened.

The Bible teaches us a lot about waiting and better yet, how to wait. Jesus waited 33 years from the point of his birth until the day of His crucifixion.

Waiting and preparation are key, and this is why it is so frequently mentioned in the Bible. Jesus knew we would have to spend some time in our lives waiting. If we think back to the plane again in the holding pattern— if the plane maintains position in the holding pattern, the remainder of the flight and the landing will be a lot smoother for everyone. How we wait does determine the outcome.

None of us know the outcome of our lives, but just like the pilot knows that the flight controller has his/her best interest at heart, we are able to stay in what may seem like a holding pattern because we know Jesus has our best interests at heart too.

I was recently driving along the motorway and was stuck behind a car going 60 kilometres per hour. Other cars were flying by me, doing the speed limit plus some. I felt like I was crawling, because I was, while others were speeding ahead. As I sat in the car that night,

I realised that was what life was feeling like at that point in time—as if I was stuck in a holding pattern.

Have you ever felt like your life was on hold? Has it ever seemed like everyone else's lives were racing ahead yet yours felt like it was at a standstill? And yet I would hate to think that I missed or gave up on inheriting the promises of God because I became impatient in the waiting.

Here we were waiting for a breakthrough, while it felt like everyone else was just motoring along with their lives. David teaches us in the book of Psalms to be still before the Lord and wait *patiently* for Him (Psalm chapter 37, verse 7). This should encourage us that sometimes we do have to wait a little bit longer than we would actually like; that waiting patiently is actually an act of obedience in following Jesus.

The second thing we ought to do is to wait *quietly* (Psalm chapter 62, verse 5). We all know and have seen people who have been waiting for something for even a short amount of time, become angry and frustrated because things aren't going in their favour. You see this when driving and at the traffic lights, let alone people who have been waiting for years for something to come to pass. More often than not, you find this type of person bitter, upset and very vocal about the injustice that they have been dealt in life. They often seem angry at the world and at God and generally, they are doing anything but waiting quietly. Yet we should remain quiet in our souls and wait patiently for Him to breakthrough for us.

The third thing we ought to do is to wait *expectantly* (Psalm chapter 130, verse 5). There are people who have grown impatient, frustrated and felt injustice, but there are also people who become despondent, dismayed and depressed that the thing they have been waiting on hasn't yet come to pass. However, as David writes in Psalm chapter 130 verse 5, we should wait with eager anticipation and hope in our hearts. We should be willing and ready for God to move. As it says in Habakkuk chapter 2 verse 3, visions await appointed times—meaning that, just because your promise hasn't come to pass yet, doesn't mean that it won't.

We must remind ourselves that we are not always going to be in a holding pattern. At one point or another the plane will land. A plane is not designed to stay in a holding pattern forever. A holding pattern is only ever temporary to clear the path ahead. Eventually the plane will come down. Whatever you are walking through right now is only temporary. You will receive your breakthrough!

The other lesson that I learnt in this season is that when you are in a holding pattern, you have to overcome the temptation to compare. We need to trust that Jesus, our flight controller, has our best interests at heart.

Each of us need to learn how to run in our own lane and accept the fact that everybody's lane looks different. Some lanes are straight, others may be curvy, others have a mountain to run over or hurdle to jump over later down the track.

I used to run cross-country at school and some days the conditions were not favourable at all. It could be raining and windy and yet, despite the conditions that you actually had no control over, you could still choose to run your best race. To me this is all that Jesus is asking of you and I. So, stop looking to your right and left and simply focus on what lays ahead of you that Jesus wants you to grab a hold of. We each have specific tasks and assignments given to us to complete.

It is so very tempting to compare your life when you feel it is at a stand-still, whether that be your career, relationships, family. You may not even compare it to others, you may just compare it to where you thought you would be in life right now. Theodore Roosevelt said that 'comparison is the thief of joy'. When you're in a stand-still, you cannot afford to lose your joy.

Always remember that your breakthrough might be just around the corner! If you are feeling like your life is on hold, cheer up, take courage—wait for Him to *breakthrough* for you (Psalm chapter 31, verse 24).

Chapter 10

NEW WINE CALLS FOR A NEW WINESKIN

However, as it is written: "What no eye has seen, what no ear has heard, and what no human mind has conceived" —the things God has prepared for those who love him— (1 Corinthians 2:9 NIV)

Every difficulty or thing we experience draws something different out of us and it requires something different from us. It produces new feelings and emotions. It challenges our faith, our prayer life and sometimes our very being. It helps us to reassess our priorities, our life perspective, our values, and stretches our physical, emotional and mental capacity. It can expose our vulnerabilities and some of our deepest insecurities. It forces us to confront our fears or run from them. It reminds us of our need for help AKA our dependency on God and others. In essence, difficult experiences force us to change.

The very definition of insanity is doing the same thing over and over again and expecting a different result.

Well, I knew we couldn't keep doing the same thing. I also knew what God was asking of me in this next season was going to be challenging (physically, mentally and emotionally).

At the beginning of 2018 I felt like God was wanting to, figuratively speaking, give me a 'New Wine Skin.' Matthew writes in Matthew chapter 9, verse 17 (NIV):

> Neither do people pour new wine into old wineskins. If they do, the skins will burst; the wine will run out and the wineskins will be ruined. No, they pour new wine into new wineskins, and both are preserved.

As new wine is more highly oxygenated, it cannot be poured into an old wine skin otherwise it will burst the old wine skin. This is due to the old wine skin having less elasticity. New skins were required to contain the new wine. To provide a little context to this particular Scripture, scholars speak about the fact that many were unfamiliar to the ways of old, so they were able to easily accept the new teaching of Jesus Christ. Hence a new wine skin was required to contain the new thing God was doing.

In order to contain the new, sometimes we have to let go of the old.

If God truly does want to do more than we can ask or imagine, then we too need to adapt, change and be prepared for it to happen so that we can contain all that He has for us. This was our story—I could not keep repeating what we had already tried because, clearly, that was not working.

PROMISE KEEPER

What I have found in my own life is that God has more to do in me before He can do more through me.

For some it may be a little less risky and more comfortable to remain where they are, rather than growing and stretching to prepare for the new.

> Increase is coming, so enlarge your tent and add extensions to your dwelling. Hold nothing back! Make the tent ropes longer and the pegs stronger.
> (Isaiah chapter 54, verse 2 TPT)

God has so much more for us!

What held the Israelites back from experiencing the promised land? Was it old thought patterns, a weak faith? An inability to see?

It is uncomfortable to recognise our own weaknesses, to confront our fears and struggles head on, to come to terms with the fact that we need help. It's a decision to be courageous, to let go of the old and grab a hold of the new.

In the book of Numbers, chapter 13, we see the Lord tell Moses to send spies in to spy out the land of Canaan. There were twelve spies who investigated the land.

In the book of Numbers chapter 13, verses 30-33 (NLT):

> But Caleb quieted the people before Moses and said, "Let us go up at once and occupy it, for we are well able to overcome it." Then the men who had gone up with him said, "We are not able to go up against the people, for they are stronger than we are." So they

brought to the people of Israel a bad report of the land that they had spied out, saying, "The land, through which we have gone to spy it out, is a land that devours its inhabitants, and all the people that we saw in it are of great height. And there we saw the Nephilim (the sons of Anak, who come from the Nephilim), and we seemed to ourselves like grasshoppers, and so we seemed to them."

Here we see the people in despair, asking "why would God send us only to fall by the sword, wouldn't we have been better in Egypt?" So here they stand between the old wine skin—representing Egypt, and the new wine skin—Canaan, 'the land flowing with milk and honey', and Joshua pipes up and says, "I reckon God could do it. If He delights in us, he will bring us into this land and will give it to us. The Lord is with us; do not fear them" (paraphrased from Numbers chapter 14, verse 8).

They stood in the present—between the past and the promised. Interesting to note that not everyone was willing to go with them into the promised land.

I don't want to be stuck in the old, I want God to do a new thing through me, in my family.

> Fling wide, you ageless doors of destiny! Here he comes; the King of Glory is ready to come in.
> (Psalm chapter 24, verse 9 TPT)

God is ready and willing to do something new in us, we just need to open our hearts and minds to what He wants to do in and through us.

I want to believe in a God that does the miraculous.

PROMISE KEEPER

David says in Psalm chapter 77, verse 14 (NIV):

> You are the God who performs miracles; you display your power among the peoples.

If I am going to believe this about God, then I'd better think bigger myself.

New Wine Skin brings New Power

Jesus says in John chapter 16, verse 33, "But take heart! I have overcome the world." If He has overcome the world, then we are certainly able to overcome any situation we are facing.

I remember praying, "Lord, I'll need you more than ever for what we are about to go through". Thankfully God did more in me, so that he could do something new through me. I'm grateful that I wasn't so stuck in my old ways of doing things that I couldn't change or grow. I wanted to be found willing and ready so that I could hold the blessing that He was about to give me.

Isaiah chapter 43, verse 19 (NIV):

> See, I am doing a new thing! Now it springs up; do you not perceive it? I am making a way in the wilderness and streams in the wasteland.

What is the new place that He is trying to take you to? What is the new thing that He is trying to do in your life?

Chapter 11

A DOUBLE BLESSING

*Instead of shame and dishonour,
you will enjoy a double share of honour.
You will possess a double portion of prosperity in
your land, and everlasting joy will be yours.
(Isaiah 61:7 NLT)*

Daniel would often have the opportunity to drive our church's guest speakers around which would also involve borrowing a friend's Toyota Prado. So, instead of driving our little Hyundai i-20, which wasn't very suitable for guests, he got to drive a new Toyota Prado and I continued driving my little white Toyota corolla (that Daniel would call my 'grannie' car). Daniel would always tell me how nice the Toyota Prado was to drive and one time he even wanted to show it to me before he returned it—he clearly wanted one. I told Daniel he would be wasting his time because, as if we could ever afford a Toyota Prado!

Then one night as we were walking our guest speakers back to the Prado, I'd realised I had parked our little Hyundai i-20 right next to them (we met there). The guest speaker asked if they were both our cars and we replied, "Oh gosh no! No, the Prado doesn't belong to us." I got in our little four-cylinder Hyundai and drove home.

The following day between church services, the couple prayed for us and began to prophecy that we would need to get a bigger car and that we would have more children. Daniel and I said a big Amen! At the start of that year, 2017, we had wanted to replace both small cars, but weren't sure how it was ever going to happen.

Shortly after, we drove another guest speaker—this time we actually had to drive him in my 'grannie' car. I have no idea why we did that to be honest. But then he went on to mention over dinner how impressed he was that we humbly drove such a car. Daniel and I laughed later on and we said to one another, "we aren't driving these cars because we are humble. We are driving them because we don't have another option!"

In August of 2017 we were on a cruise when I clearly felt the Holy Spirit impress upon me to believe for a 7-seater car. I remember telling Daniel and feeling like I was crazy, as at that point we had only been believing to get a slightly bigger car. Daniel said, "Babe, I know we are believing for more children but a 7-seater car... really?"

I replied, "yep, that's what I honestly feel like God has said and for us to do anything else would be disobedient." Then I personally questioned why we would need a 7-seater car. Daniel responded, "and even if we got a 7-seater car there is no way we could afford insurance and registration on a bigger car."

A couple of months passed and we now had my

sister's family living with us. They were in the process of preparing to move to South Africa which meant they were selling off all they had, including their two vehicles. That's right, there were four adults and three small children living in our tiny three-bedroom townhouse. Fortunately, however, we still had our two cars which meant they were able to borrow one of them.

In October of 2017 I was driving my sister home late one night after a women's event and, as we were driving through an intersection on a green light, another woman ran a red light and hit my side of the car. Amazingly, my sister and I walked away injury free, however, my "grannie" car was a total write-off. So now both my sister's family and our family were down to one car—our little Hyundai i-20. We had been believing to replace both cars, but now we actually needed to. So, Daniel and I tried to be obedient and believe for a 7-seater car, but every time we would even enquire about a second-hand car that we liked, it had already been sold. One morning we were about to leave to drive two hours to pick up the car we had said to the owner that we would purchase. As we were getting ready to go, the owner sent us a text saying she had already sold it the night before.

Then on one Saturday night in early January around 9pm, we had a missed call from someone. It was a little unusual, especially considering how late it was, so we called them back. That was a very good decision! They were calling to let us know that they were gifting us a brand-new car! They went on to say how they had wanted to purchase a brand-new Toyota Prado; they'd felt like they had the okay from God and so they went ahead with it. They'd decided on all the extra fittings and colour, but as they were finalising it all, they felt the Holy Spirit whisper to them, "you will buy it, but you will never drive it. This car is for Daniel and Elise".

To this day I can't imagine what they were thinking when they felt the Holy Spirit say this to them, but nonetheless, they proceeded to inform us that in three days' time, we could drive to Sunshine Toyota in Currimundi on the Sunshine Coast, and pick up our brand-new Toyota Prado! Oh, and there was one more thing—they wanted to pay for the registration and insurance for the next seven years!

We had not spoken to anyone that we wanted a Toyota Prado, let alone how we felt about paying for insurance and registration. I was so grateful to God and just couldn't believe of the kindness of our God. I then realised that, back in August when God began to share His heart with me about us having a 7-seater car, He would also be speaking with the person whom he could do it through.

A few days after we had picked up the beautiful, brand new car, Daniel was driving home and he felt the Holy Spirit say to Him, "don't just believe that God would add one car to your family... you were praying for two." A week later almost to the day, we sat down with a family who had asked to meet with us. We knew this family but hadn't caught up in a little while. They told us that they too had once been given a diagnosis that they couldn't have children of their own, but God had gifted them with two beautiful children.

They sat there and prophesied over us and our church that day with the very Scripture I shared with you earlier and, as an act of faith and obedience, gifted us their Nissan X-trail. The gentleman said that three years ago when they saw me putting our pram into our car, they felt the Holy Spirit encourage them, "Would you give your car to Dan and Elise?" He replied, "when we pay it off I will Lord". Three years later they gifted us their car. We were shocked, humbled and ecstatic.

At this point in my life I'd seen God move, but not like this. I remember hearing old stories of God doing things like this in others' lives, but couldn't quite get over the fact that He was still able to perform such miracles today.

I'm not sure what you are currently walking through as you read this, but I pray that you would receive a double portion of prosperity in your land!

Chapter 12

THE SCARE

You intended to harm me, but God intended it all for good. (Genesis 50:20 NLT)

On Boxing Day of 2017, I woke up with pain in my abdomen. I didn't think much of it, assuming I had eaten too much at Christmas Day lunch the day before. The next day that pain in my abdomen became sharper and I knew something was wrong. I packed a hospital bag and Daniel drove me to the hospital.

It turned out to be appendicitis and within two hours of arriving at the hospital, I was in theatre having an appendectomy. A couple of weeks later I was back in the outpatient clinic awaiting my follow-up appointment. I remember that day because I had to wait an hour and a half for my appointment. As I was waiting, I looked down and ran my finger over a charm on my bracelet that read—you've got this. I did not realise the significance of that moment until sometime later. I walked into the surgeon's office and sat down. He said he was happy with how the surgery went and asked about my recovery.

The surgeon went on to tell me that the pathology results showed that there was a neuroendocrine tumour in my appendix. He reassured me that they had removed the tumour without realising it when they removed my appendix.

He explained that these types of tumours were usually intact, but when learning of my ripe family history of cancer, he sent me for further investigation. I was a little shocked walking out, as I didn't know what this all meant. I wished I had taken someone with me to that appointment.

Thankfully, I went to see my general practitioner shortly after and he went through it all with me, explaining that I had a stage 1 active cancerous tumour growing in my appendix. He did say, had it not been removed, in seven to ten years it would have caused me a lot of trouble.

I was completely shocked—cancer, I'm 31 I thought! My second thought was, what a miracle it was that they removed it. Praise God I didn't even know that I had it. My third thought—is there more of it in my system? My fourth thought was—what does this mean for our family, will we have more children?

Fear immediately tried to overtake me. This is when 2 Corinthians chapter 10, verse 5 came to my mind:

> ...we take captive every thought to make it obedient to Christ. (NIV)

I remember coming home that day and telling Daniel that it was indeed cancerous. That wasn't the nicest day as the fear of the unknown can be somewhat debilitating. I immediately went for a CT scan of my abdomen. The wait for the results was terrible but praise God they came back all clear!

I just wanted to get on with our lives and our dream of having another baby, but at another follow up appointment from my CT scan, the surgeon strongly said to me, "As important as your family is to you, so your health should be as well". This was a bit of a kick up the butt. So, we put everything else on hold to ensure my body was all clear. Even though my CT scan came back clear, my surgeon wanted me to have a colonoscopy done as well.

It was then that I attended Hillsong's Colour Conference, a women's conference in Sydney, which was really perfect timing. I remember moments in worship honestly questioning if we would ever have more children and fearing if I had cancer growing in other parts of my body. At this particular conference, there was basically an entire session dedicated to taking communion together and praying over one another. Again, I was so blessed to be surrounded by such incredible women of faith who decided to pray over me. We stood and prayed, and I wept, and we took communion together and declared God's healing power in my life.

When I returned home, we continued to take communion every morning. We thanked Jesus for the bread that represents His body that was broken so that ours could be made whole, and thanked Him for the juice that represents His blood that was shed for the forgiveness of our sins. I continued to declare His power at work in my body.

In the book of Acts chapter 3 verse 6 (NIV), Peter

says:

> Silver or gold I do not have, but what I do have I give you. In the name of Jesus Christ of Nazareth, walk.

I love this story, because we see here a lame man who is expecting to receive silver or gold, not realising that what Jesus actually wanted to do through Peter was to make him whole. Verse 7 goes onto say:

> Taking him by the right hand, Peter helped him up. And at once the man's feet and ankles were strengthened.

Every day I began to pray and would command my body—in the name of Jesus Christ of Nazareth, be whole.

Well, at my follow up appointment following the colonoscopy, my doctor told me that the biopsy they had taken near the site where the tumour was removed was 100% clear, meaning that, like my surgeon had originally thought—the tumour had remained intact and I was completely healthy. That was a good day! To be honest, I was overwhelmed by His goodness in our lives.

I really couldn't quite believe it—that as a result of having appendicitis, a cancerous tumour had been removed in my body before we were even aware of it. Thank you Jesus! The fact that I cannot get life insurance cover for another 10 years is a minor thing compared to the fact that it was found early.

Genesis chapter 50, verse 20 (NLT):

PROMISE KEEPER

You intended to harm me, but God intended it all for good.

Regardless of the situations in our lives we ought to keep declaring His Word over our situation and thank Him for His faithfulness.

Chapter 13

BOW ONCE

I was young and now I am old,
yet I have never seen the righteous forsaken
or their children begging bread.
(Psalm 37:25 NIV)

In August of 2017 we were on a P&O Cruise around the Pacific Islands when I felt like the Holy Spirit had given me an idea for a sermon. I certainly wasn't thinking about a preaching topic; I knew I had to preach at church in a couple of months' time, but it was like I literally woke up one morning and the Holy Spirit downloaded the Scripture and points. The irony though, was that in the next couple of days, I would have to live out the sermon first before preaching it. On day six of the cruise I began to miscarry again, now for the 4th time. It was certainly not what I had planned, but this was where this chapter was birthed.

In the book of Daniel chapter 3, Shadrach, Meshach and Abednego appeared before King Nebuchadnezzar because they refused to bow down before him. Upon King Nebuchadnezzar's second request, Shadrach, Meshach and Abednego replied:

> King Nebuchadnezzar, we do not need to defend ourselves before you in this matter. If we are thrown into the blazing furnace, the God we serve is able to deliver us from it, and he will deliver us from Your Majesty's hand. But even if he does not, we want you to know, Your Majesty, that we will not serve your gods or worship the image of gold you have set up. (Daniel chapter 3, verses 16-18 NIV)

Here we have Shadrach, Meshach and Abednego faced with the very prospect of losing their own lives. And not for any other reason than for standing up for what they believed in.

Shadrach, Meshach and Abednego were saying, "It is not that we won't bow down, it is that we can't bow down". Since they had already bowed down in their soul to God, they could not bow again to the image of gold. They understood that you can only bow once; that in life we either bow to God or to popular opinion, social acceptance, what everyone else is doing, or to the image of gold.

You can bow once but you can't bow twice.

Within this story we see King Nebuchadnezzar erect a golden image of himself. Scholars say that it was so large it exceeded the ordinary stature of a man fifteen times. King Nebuchadnezzar called forth all officials, governors, treasurers, judges, magistrates. As far as the eye could see people were bowing down, apparently three million in fact.

And here we have a man who tells King Nebuchadnezzar, that three of his men who oversee the provinces of Babylon refuse to bow down. King Nebuchadnezzar, a king used to getting his own way, threatens again by making the furnace seven times hotter, and yet they still don't bow.

Think about it—if you were there standing before King Nebuchadnezzar what would you do? I think, more than likely, I would find an excuse, something along the lines of: *everyone else is doing it...it's just once...I will pretend to bow—but God knows my heart...I will bow today but ask for God's forgiveness tomorrow...It's just a bow...I have prayed about it, and I think it's culturally relevant...I will only do it once, it's not like I am going to create a habit out of it.*

For Shadrach, Meshach and Abednego it wasn't that they wouldn't bow down, it was that they couldn't bow. They had made the decision to bow once to God. They knew what bowing twice would mean.

To bow twice is to worship disobedience.

Shadrach, Meshach and Abednego realised that they would either be worshipping disobedience by bowing down and worshipping this gold image; or be obedient to the Lord and be tied up and thrown into the fiery furnace—which was so hot that even the soldiers who would throw them into the furnace would die of the heat. What a proposition to be faced with!

Think about what these three men were risking if

they decided not to bow down to King Nebuchadnezzar, it wasn't like they were nobodies. They had leadership roles in overseeing the provinces of Babylon. They were risking stature, position and authority amongst their colleagues and earthly King.

But isn't this always the case when we are either obedient to what we know Jesus is asking of us—which may seem uncommon to the natural eye. Or disobedient to what we know is true?

I know I do this, probably a little too often, only to realise—I should have listened when I felt a gentle nudge to do the exact opposite.

> I don't really understand myself, for I want to do what is right, but I don't do it. Instead, I do what I hate.
> (Romans chapter 7, verse 15 NLT)

In Philipians chapter 2, it says that Jesus humbled himself and became obedient even unto the death that he suffered on the cross. Now we may not all be asked to be so obedient that we die physically. But we are being asked to have such extreme obedience and trust in Jesus that we die to our own will at times, our emotions and feelings. We are to live according to His Word.

Scripture says Jesus' authority multiplied after He bowed down to His Father's will. And isn't this the case, that when you and I decide not to bow down to disobedience, not to go off and do our own thing, but instead do the very thing that He asks of us, that we experience a greater level of authority and understanding of who our God is and what He is capable of?

It is no surprise that Shadrach, Meshach and

Abednego volunteered to be thrown into the furnace—**because they knew what it was to be obedient, even unto death.**

For Shadrach, Meshach and Abednego to have this level of obedience, it wouldn't have been a once-off but rather, it was the pattern of their lives.

Obedience means accepting that His will and plan is far greater than mine. It might not look like it or seem like it right now, but it is!

It may feel like the timeline might be a little longer, my list of preconceived ideas might need to be thrown out the window, my previous list of expectations may need to go unmet for now (i.e. I thought surely I would have had a second child by now).

Disobedience says—we may 'know' better, but obedience says—His plans and His ways are far greater.

To bow twice is to worship disobedience and distrust.

Hypothetically, if these three guys were to bow again, they would have been bowing to thoughts and excuses which doubt if God is trustworthy. Is he reliable? Would he come through for them? But instead, I love the conviction of these men:

> If we are thrown into the blazing furnace, the God we serve is able to deliver us from it, and he will deliver us from Your Majesty's hand. But even if he does not, we want you to know, Your Majesty, that we will not serve your gods or worship the image of gold you have set up. (Daniel chapter 3, verses 16-18 NIV)

Essentially they are saying that they'd trust God even if he didn't come through, even if they didn't get their breakthrough. Even if their situation got worse to the natural eye—they would still trust Him.

The interesting thing to note was that, if these three men decided to worship distrust, they would never have told the story of going through the fiery furnace.

No one else got to experience this. These three men walked around in a fire with Jesus.

The reality is that we all like the idea of exhibiting the strength and tenacity of a person who has experienced or walked through a difficult situation, without actually having experienced it personally. We all want to be people with an overcoming attitude without having had to be delivered an unwelcome report. We all want to be people who persevere, who have patience and grace without having had to go through a difficult experience with someone. We all want the character traits of somebody who has stood the test of time whilst receiving everything instantly—right?

I'm sure Shadrack, Meshach and Abednego would have loved to have had the victory of coming out of the furnace without first having had to experience it.

Isn't it funny, how some people walk through really tough situations? Where perhaps they haven't had to be thrown into a fiery furnace, but they have been given an unwanted diagnosis, and the different ways they handle it? Some people become agnostic—doubt God's existence, don't care for God and stop coming to church, whilst others make the decision to trust God and walk it out with Him.

When you and I bow twice, we not only bow to

disobedience and distrust but also we worship dishonour.

For Shadrach, Meshach and Abednego, to bow twice would mean to bring shame and disgrace upon their relationship with God. But isn't this exactly what happens when we decide to bow down and worship anything but honour?

These three men would rather dishonour their earthly King, than God Almighty. They made the call that they would rather potentially bring shame and disgrace upon themselves by not bowing down to this golden image, than bring shame and humiliation upon their God.

Here is the most powerful King, and now he wants to make a public example of them for their dishonour towards him.

> For the eyes of the Lord range throughout the earth to strengthen those whose hearts are fully committed to him. (2 Chronicles chapter 16, verse 9 NIV)

When you and I bow only once, God helps us and strengthens us in our request. When you and I bow only once, we bow to honour.

I don't know if you have ever been humiliated—perhaps for what you believed in or something Jesus asked of you—but I do know that God chooses the foolish things of this world to shame the wise, and the weak to shame the strong (1 Corinthians chapter 1, verse 27).

In the book of Joshua, God instructs him how to win the battle and take back the city of Jericho.

> Then the Lord said to Joshua, "See, I have delivered Jericho into your hands, along with its king and its fighting men. March around the city once with all the armed men. Do this for six days. Have seven priests carry trumpets of rams' horns in front of the ark. On the seventh day, march around the city seven times, with the priests blowing the trumpets. When you hear them sound a long blast on the trumpets, have the whole army give a loud shout; then the wall of the city will collapse and the army will go up, everyone straight in." (Joshua chapter 6, verses 2-5 NIV)

I can imagine the officials sitting on the city gates watching the men walking around thinking, "there they go again!" No doubt they would have been laughing at them, paying out on them—"what an idiot... Does he really think all that walking will bring down these fortified walls, that are metres high?"

But God did exactly as He promised, and victory was won because Joshua honoured what God had said.

A few years ago when I was in Rome, I visited the Spanish Steps and learnt a little of the history. I found it interesting to learn that they were originally built in the 1700s to connect the Trinita dei Monti church and the Spanish square below. The French, who governed the church at that point, were also planning to erect a statue of King Louis XIV at the top of the staircase. But it never eventuated because the Pope wouldn't allow it. Perhaps it was because what he wanted people to see from the Spanish square was the church and not some statue of a King.

Honouring God may mean different things for all of us. It may be in facing some personal shame, humiliation, disgrace; standing up for what you believe, despite the opinions of others or your work colleagues, friends, university acquaintances; living a life that is worthy of honour. It might be following through with something crazy that God has asked of you, or it may be in each day, waking up and asking Jesus, "please help me to honour you today".

To bow once is to worship and honour God, but to bow twice is to worship dishonour.

Finally, we see King Nebuchadnezzar leap to his feet in amazement when he sees four men walking around in the furnace. Scripture says that the King checked with his advisors asking them, "didn't we only throw three men in?" The advisors of course, agreed. Then in King Nebuchadnezzar's amazement he says, "but I see four men walking around in there, unharmed, unbound, and the fourth looks like a son of God".

King Nebuchadnezzar then approaches them, and now refers to them as the servants of the Most High God and calls to them to come out.

When you and I bow once, we bow to obedience, trust and honour and God honours this and joins us in our fight. Here's the thing, it wasn't just about Shadrach, Meshach and Abednego. It was their faith that not only changed the heart of King Nebuchadnezzar, but also others.

You just don't know what your step of faith might mean to the other three million people that are watching.

What's going to change in your workplace, family, university or school as a result of your faith? What's going to happen because of you?

King Nebuchadnezzar goes from putting anyone who does not bow down and worship him in a heated furnace seven times hotter than normal, to making a decree that anyone who says anything against the God of Shadrach, Meshach and Abednego be cut in pieces and their houses to be turned into piles of rubble.

Unfortunately, scholars say that despite this miracle that took place and brought about deep convictions on Nebuchadnezzar—no abiding change, no long-lasting change actually took place in his conduct.

Isn't it true, people see miracles, but unless their hearts are ready and their eyes are open to see it, they will go back to their old ways.

However, here's the key—what God did for these three men would help to keep the other believers to their religion while in captivity and to cure them of idolatry.

What is it today that you need to stop bowing down to? What is it today that you need to stop making excuses for?

These three men couldn't actually bow down to anything else because they had first bowed down to God.

In this time of waiting and disappointment, I had to keep being obedient to God and following His leading. I had to keep trusting Him that He would deliver on His promise and I had to keep worshiping Him, and with that I knew He would prove Himself faithful in my

PROMISE KEEPER

life, in our lives, just like He did for Shadrach, Meshach and Abednego.

Chapter 14

IVF

Consequently, faith comes from hearing the message, and the message is heard through the word about Christ. (Romans 10:17 NIV)

I'll never forget where I was and what I was doing when I heard that soft, still voice say to me, "You need to see an infertility specialist." I had hoped that I was wrong and that we wouldn't need to. You see, naively, or perhaps it was my pride, I wanted God to perform a miracle. What I didn't realise at that point in time was that sometimes God will perform His miracle through modern day medicine. I never envisaged us going down the path of in vitro fertilization (IVF)—but I did know that God had given me a promise, and that we needed medical help.

By this stage I, along with Daniel, had seen many doctors, a natural hormone specialist and natural practitioners, however, to no avail. Then, through a funny set of circumstances, my previous general practitioner, who lived in another city 1200kms away, referred us to one of Queensland's renown infertility specialists in Brisbane. After a few weeks I finally got around to phoning up and made an appointment. It was September 2017 and we were given an appointment for the following June (2018)—we were on a 10-month waiting list. Surely, he had to be good! Upon reading reviews online, women were saying his treatments involved large amounts of medication and apparently his bed-side manner wasn't all that great, but women were seeing great success from his treatments. So here we were waiting 10 months just to see an infertility specialist.

I still had my doubts and a lot of uncertainty around going down this particular path—it was new to me, it was new to us. For some reason, I thought that it was the wrong thing to do, that going down this path wasn't trusting in God. As a believer, was this okay?

Fortunately, through the weekly women's meeting that I was leading at the time, I started speaking with the mother of a daughter who had recently given birth to a baby who was helped to be conceived through IVF, in the same conversation was another woman who also conceived their last child with IVF. I had told them what I felt God had been speaking to me, and they shared Scriptures with me; Scriptures they felt God had given them in regards to going down this path. How good is it when you talk things through with others and get God's perspective on the situation at hand? Faith certainly does come by hearing the Word of God.

There were many times before we saw our specialist that I would feel so frustrated that our situation hadn't changed, yet God was so good and kind to us in this waiting. Just a few days before Christmas, we received a phone call from a nurse at the infertility clinic—we called it our early Christmas present. She was calling regarding the appointment that I had made, to notify us that there had been a cancellation on the doctor's very last appointment before they closed for the Christmas break and to ask if we would like it? So, instead of waiting another six months for an appointment, I only had to wait another 22 hours! We were ecstatic to say the least, finally we felt like there was a way forward.

> I am making a way in the wilderness and streams in the wasteland. (Isaiah chapter 43 verse 19 NIV)

I remember that appointment because it all felt so new, in time it would become very familiar. As we entered the clinic, we carried our promise in our hearts, but also knew the road ahead wasn't going to be easy. We explained our history, and the specialist explained that he was unsure why we kept having recurrent miscarriages. It could be a number of different things, he said.

The specialist discovered more endometriosis and he wanted it removed before we started the first round of treatment. I had only had the last operation to remove the Endometriosis in April of 2017, we were now in December of 2017. So, I was booked in for an operation to have it removed late January 2018. We did leave that appointment with hope, as he was willing to try anything and everything he could to make our promise a reality. As we left, we saw our specialist join the Christmas party and felt extremely thankful knowing that he could have chosen to finish up early that day, but instead, God had made a way for us to meet with him.

How good it was to start the new year with a

detailed plan in mind. We were very grateful.

A week after we met with him was when I was going into hospital and ended up having my appendix removed—along with the tumour. Then four weeks almost to the day after that, I was back having the endometriosis removed. Two operations in four weeks! I felt like the wind had been taken out of me and all I wanted to do was to have children and get on with life.

Immediately after the endometriosis was removed, we were to start treatment. The next five months consisted of many appointments, blood tests, medications and injections. Infertility treatment is one of those interesting things because it is extremely private and yet, all consuming. We not only wanted to fall pregnant, but we obviously wanted to stay pregnant, so perhaps that's why for us the treatment was even more intense.

After a couple of failed attempts of Intrauterine Insemination (IUI) we'd felt led to try a round of IVF. I suppose like anything in life, you cannot treat something until you are prepared and willing to uncover a myriad of other things. The further we went along this path, the more issues our specialist discovered. Thankfully, there were very supportive and empathetic nurses who honestly made me feel like they were on the journey with me. For the first time, I felt like I not only had people that loved us and wanted the best for us, but we also had a team of experts surrounding us.

As I sat in the recovery room, having had the egg retrieval completed for our first round of Intracytoplasmic Sperm Injection (ICSI), I had the opportunity to meet and talk with three other women who were all going through IVF. Unlike myself, who was so new at this, most had been through this at least two times before—some even more. I prayed as I sat there and watched the clinical embryologist approach each woman and explain to them how the procedure had gone and any preliminary findings they had on the embryos. We were doing a fresh transfer which meant our embryologist would insert my good, mature looking eggs with one of Daniel's sperm immediately.

Out of the 17 eggs that were removed, eight of them were deemed mature but only three of them fertilized overnight. Over the next four days, as I recovered from that procedure, I called every day to check how our little embryos were going. They needed to get to a Stage 5 Blastocyte in order to be implanted on the sixth day. Things weren't looking particularly good each day when I called. But then on the sixth day at 5am, I received the phone call from the specialist telling us to come straight down to Brisbane as one of them had progressed to an early blastocyte stage. Praise God!

We had our little embryo implanted and then off we went. The following week I went for a blood test and, well hello, my results showed that I was indeed pregnant! As per normal procedure, we went for another blood test seven days later. That afternoon I received a pretty upsetting phone call. The nurse from the specialists' rooms told me my levels had all dropped and now were indicating I was anything but pregnant. They referred to it as a biochemical pregnancy. I was devastated to say the least. We had invested a lot, emotionally, physically, and financially. Even the nurses told me how unusual it is only to have one embryo out of 17 eggs that were retrieved.

It was now June (2018) and we had organised a trip away to beautiful Mission Beach in Tropical North Queensland for my brother's wedding. It was perfect timing and a great distraction. We decided to keep on trusting God, and found comfort in this Scripture:

> That is why I am suffering as I am. Yet there is no cause for shame, because I know whom I have believed and am convinced that he is able to guard what I have entrusted to him until that day.
> (2 Timothy chapter 1, verse 12 NIV)

We had a promise for a little girl, but we would continue to place our trust in Jesus—that he would guard it until it became a reality for us. While we were away, I had to call our specialists rooms to make a follow up appointment, following our recent negative pregnancy blood test. It was during this follow up phone call that the receptionist informed me that our infertility specialist was retiring at the end of the year.

Though I was disappointed with this news, I realised that meant we mustn't have needed his wisdom anymore. Thank goodness for faith-filled people in your life, especially when you are not feeling so faith-filled. We had done everything we could in the natural, left the rest up to God, and here we were back where we started.

It was around this time when Daniel woke up one morning and said he had felt like the Holy Spirit had spoken to him saying that "Faith doesn't dangle it's promises, it delivers on them." Even though we felt we had now exhausted all of our options, Jesus was giving us even greater assurance that He would deliver on His promise.

David wrote in Psalm chapter 40 verse 3 (NLT):

> He has given me a new song to sing, a hymn of praise to our God. Many will see what he has done and be amazed. They will put their trust in the Lord.

We knew that God had not only given us this promise, but that in delivering it, it would encourage others to keep believing for their miracle too. Not long after this, one of my friends told me that her husband thought we would fall pregnant naturally. At this stage I honestly didn't believe that this was possible. I mean, we had fallen pregnant naturally but had also miscarried as well, aside from Jonathan of course.

Even so, one afternoon I walked into our study where our bookshelf is, and picked up a book that a kind friend had given me before Jonathan was born. I started reading and couldn't put it down. It was about a woman and her husband who had been told it would be very difficult for them to conceive after being diagnosed with various things. However, she just refused to believe what was said and instead, decided to stand on the Word of God who promises that we will multiply, that we would not be barren, nor would we miscarry (Ezekiel chapter 23, verse 26).

A couple of weeks later while my husband was in South Africa on a ministry trip, my sister came with me to my follow up appointment. The specialist didn't sound super positive in moving forward—he was unsure why it hadn't worked for us and why I didn't have any other embryos to freeze and use for a later time. He said we could either just walk or try one more type of treatment. It was far more invasive and even more intense than the last. I wondered how that was possible, until he started describing the different drugs and hormone treatments I would be on.

However, we felt like we had one more go with this specialist (before he retired) so we ought to give it a go. At the end of the conversation, after this specialist had listed all the different things that Daniel and I had now been diagnosed with, he ended with the words "But…It's not impossible." Those four words were enough, and my sister insisted, out of the entire depressing conversation that I remember, that I hold onto and declare those four words over myself.

We went home and I started the injections again in preparation to start treatment the following month. We felt like God had led us this far, so why not give it one more go?

How many times do we feel to do something, yet in the natural it seems that the opposite is happening? Matthew writes in Matthew chapter 19, verse 26 (NIV):

> With man this is impossible, but with God all things are possible.

All things, even those that don't look or seem it!

No wonder why God teaches us in Joshua chapter 1, verse 2, to be strong and courageous. He knows the near impossibilities that we will face and that we will need strength and courage to push on and keep believing.

I also had to be reminded of His power. David writes in Psalm chapter 46, verse 6 (TPT):

> When the nations are in uproar with their tottering kingdoms God simply raises His voice and the Earth begins to disintegrate before Him.

We serve a powerful God who is truly able to do anything.

No one suddenly decides that they want to do IVF. It is only really a path you go down when you can't have children on your own, or is a wiser option due to genetic predispositions. For us, we had a plan of things to try and it was the very last thing on our list. When we had ticked off all others and felt led to try IVF—we went with it.

If you are currently undergoing some type of fertility treatment, my heart goes out to you. It is certainly not for the faint-hearted. I pray today for courage, for peace, for rest and for great support to come around you and encourage you—don't give up, keep on believing!

Your miracle is on its way.

Chapter 15

FROM SMALL THINGS BIG THINGS GROW

"Truly I tell you, if you have faith as small as a mustard seed, you can say to this mountain, 'Move from here to there,' and it will move. Nothing will be impossible for you." (Matthew 17:20 NLT)

Never despise the day of the small beginnings.

I have often found that this is how dreams begin; they do not arrive in their completed state but rather, they start as something small—yet significant. Perhaps it begins with a thought, a vision, a word, and with time it expands, layers are added until finally and all of a sudden, it arrives in all its fullness.

Our promise of having another child was like this. In April of 2015, right before our first miscarriage, I had a vision of a little girl. Over the following years, as time passed, many beautiful layers including greater detail of this little girl were added. With each disappointment and setback in the natural, the promise, funnily enough, became clearer. Each statement of fear or doubt made by someone well-meaning, further cemented the promise that God had given me. I'm certainly no superwoman. After every comment of fear or doubt, I would go and measure it up against what God had already said to me.

It wasn't long after our second miscarriage, I was thinking of this quote, 'from small things, big things grow.' I actually uploaded it on my social media account and had people text me shortly after asking if I was pregnant. I wasn't expecting in the natural, however I carried a deeper, more detailed promise in my heart. One that was unseen to others, but not to Daniel and I.

Have you ever felt like that? When God has so clearly spoken to you, not everyone may be able to see it or understand, but you can? Overtime we had many different people share with us visions that they had of us with a little girl, prophetic words over her life including what she would do and how God was going to use her.

In the book of Matthew, chapter 17, Jesus heals a demon possessed boy. In verses 19-21, the disciples ask Him in private:

> "Why couldn't we cast out that demon?"
> "You don't have enough faith," Jesus told them. "I tell you the truth, if you had faith even as small as a mustard seed, you could say to this mountain, 'Move from here to there,' and it would move. Nothing would be impossible." (NLT)

I believe in a God that moves mountains; I need to believe in a God that can! Perhaps you just need to repeat this to yourself today—my God can move mountains.

Do you believe in a God that can move the

mountains in your life?
David writes in Psalm chapter 24 verses 1-2 (TPT):

> God claims the world as his. Everything and everyone belongs to him! He's the one who pushed back oceans to let the dry ground appear, planting firm foundations for the earth.

Over the courses of our fertility treatment, I began to frequently speak this out over my body; that if the God I serve can push back oceans to let dry ground appear, then He can certainly heal my body and make it carry a baby to full term.

Then in April of 2018 at a women's evening held at our church, our guest speaker, Ps Leanne Matthesius, prophesied over me that a blessing was going to come to my womb and that there would be miracles in this house (the church). This was another layer. At the end of church the next morning, I had a beautiful friend hand me a gift, a gift they had felt to buy me—and so she handed them to me in faith. The gift was a beautifully knitted pair of little girl booties. Our promise was further strengthened, and again, the timing was perfect.

> You are the God who performs miracles; you display your power among the peoples.
> (Psalm chapter 77 verse 14 NIV)

Your current condition or situation is not too great for Him.

Don't give up on your promise from God. As I write this chapter of the book, I am still waiting for ours to come to pass. Perhaps it hasn't happened yet because it won't give the most glory to God yet. Or perhaps it's because this promise has an appointed time attached to it—for a specific purpose. Or perhaps God is looking to strengthen you first. What I do know is that our God is a good God and like any father, He doesn't withhold good gifts from His kids.

If you are believing for a child and you haven't felt like God has given you a specific vision or word, just remember, the only promise you need is found in the book of Genesis, chapter 9 verse 7 where God instructs us to go forth and multiply. At any point that our bodies are not doing this, then they are not being obedient to the Word of God.

All we need is a small amount of faith and belief that with God, anything is possible!

Write down who will be affected, encouraged, grateful and inspired to believe for more, when you receive your promise. This will greatly encourage you to keep going. Keep putting one foot in front of the other. Keep rejoicing because you have the promise, and you too will see it come to pass.

Chapter 16

COME WITH ME

The fig tree forms its early fruit; the blossoming vines spread their fragrance. Arise, come, my darling; my beautiful one, come with me.
(Song of Solomon 2:13 NIV)

Jesus' desire is for you and I to live a life of abundance and one that is overflowing. We achieve this by deciding to trust in Him and follow His leading.

I hear the Lord saying, "I will stay close to you, instructing and guiding you along the pathway for your life. I will advise you along the way and lead you forth with my eyes as your guide. So don't make it difficult; don't be stubborn when I take you where you've not been before. Don't make me tug you and pull you along. Just come with me!" (Psalm 32:6-9 TPT)

I first heard this translation at Colour Conference in March 2018. It resonated with me because this is how I had imagined Jesus speaking to me, firmly but with warmth.

I have read Matthew chapter 14 quite a few times where Jesus instructs Peter to step out of the boat, and then we read of Peter walking on water. I've heard the story preached many times but never envisaged the way that Jesus was actually speaking to Peter in this instance.

Matthew chapter 14, verse 22-30 (NIV):

> Immediately Jesus made the disciples get into the boat and go on ahead of him to the other side, while he dismissed the crowd. After he had dismissed them, he went up on a mountainside by himself to pray. Later that night, he was there alone, and the boat was already a considerable distance from land, buffeted by the waves because the wind was against it.
> Shortly before dawn Jesus went out to them, walking on the lake. When the disciples saw him walking on the lake, they were terrified. "It's a ghost," they said, and cried out in fear.
> But Jesus immediately said to them: "Take courage! It is I. Don't be afraid."
> "Lord, if it's you," Peter replied, "tell me to come to you on the water."
> "Come," he said.
> Then Peter got down out of the boat, walked on the water and came toward Jesus. But when he saw the wind, he was afraid and, beginning to sink, cried out, "Lord, save me!"

For the first time, instead of imagining Jesus yelling at Peter to get out of the boat, to COME, I saw it as a quiet but authoritative 'come.' Because they were already in relationship, Jesus trusted Peter and Peter trusted Jesus. And Peter knew if he was to follow Jesus' leading he would not be worse off, that it would be okay, that it would be safe.

As we began seeking further medical help with our infertility specialist, I would continually hear this soft, still voice—"Come."

When you know who is leading you, you're okay with the way forward. We may not understand it, nor could we comprehend all that was going on, but we trust in the person that does.

1 Corinthians chapter 10, verse 13 (AMP) says:

> No temptation [regardless of its source] has overtaken or enticed you that is not common to human experience [nor is any temptation unusual or beyond human resistance]; but God is faithful [to His word— He is compassionate and trustworthy], and He will not let you be tempted beyond your ability [to resist], but along with the temptation He [has in the past and is now and] will [always] provide the way out as well, so that you will be able to endure it [without yielding, and will overcome temptation with joy].

We can follow Jesus' leading because He never gives us more than we can handle.

How nice is it to know when and where you are going somewhere, how long it's going to take? How nice is it to feel in control and know every single detail?

In 2010 I went to Europe for a few week's

holiday; I was meeting family there but flew over by myself. It was my first overseas flight alone and so naturally I was feeling a little apprehensive to start with. I remember sitting on the plane knowing that we had a stopover in Abu Dhabi. That part was fine but then all of a sudden mid-flight we began to descend. I turned to the older gentleman who was sitting beside me and asked him if he knew why we were descending? He had no clue, I looked at the map on the screen and it didn't say that we were stopping anywhere. When we landed, the air hostesses just told us to take all of our hand luggage off the plane and be back in 30 minutes as they had to refuel. It was just past midnight and I was walking off the plane asking people where we were.

Like most, I actually really like the feeling of knowing where I am going, what to expect. Yet that type of life doesn't require much faith.

Romans chapter 1, verse 17 (NKJV) says that, 'The just shall live by faith'. Our lives, our jobs, our families would be lifeless if we were always in control and knew how things were going to end.

I want to be a big spirited person who lives by faith, who believes for more for my own life and others. In the same way, I want to see others breakthrough, people healed and made whole. Therefore, I am totally fine with not knowing it all so that this can happen. But it does mean continually choosing to put our trust in Jesus and release that need for control to Him.

Recently I was driving with our five-year-old son and he loves to be able to see where we are going. In one of our cars we have an inbuilt map and the other one we do not. When we drive in the car without the in-built map he asks for my phone so that he can put the map application on and tell me where to go. On this particular day, I was driving him to his Kindergarten, so I didn't need the map because I knew where I was going. But he insisted for it to be on so that he could see where we were going—yes, we have a determined son and I love that!

As we mature as Christians, we come to learn that if our heavenly Father knows where we are going, then we don't necessarily need to know every detail or be able to see every turn. We simply learn to walk by faith and follow His leading.

Like any good, kind and caring father encouraging you along the way—just go with Him, follow Him, take His hand, put your trust in Him. Don't make it difficult for Him, don't be stubborn, 'Just come.'

Time and time again, even with every painful injection or medication taken (because I really dislike taking tablets full stop), I would hear this soft, still voice encouraging me along the way—"Just wait until you hold her…Just wait until you see her," and I would think how special it will be to see Daniel holding a little girl. It mightn't be easy, but it'll be worth it.

Just go with Him, whatever that looks like for you today I know you will be greatly rewarded!

Chapter 17

THE POWER OF SAYING YES

Let it be to me according to your word.
(Luke 1:37-38 NKJV)

Have you ever said yes to something without fully comprehending what you were saying yes to? Raising a child is a lot like this. Parenthood is quite possibly the most unprepared, unqualified thing that you could ever do in your life, even when you have people around you that have gone before. No one can quite give you an accurate heads-up of what is to come and, even if their advice is reasonably accurate, your child will, no doubt, be somewhat different to theirs.

In the gospel of Luke, we see a young teenage girl named Mary. She lived in an unimportant town at that time called Nazareth, a town in the hills of Galilee. Mary, although less privileged, was from a good family.

She loved God and had been taught the Scriptures from a young age. Having known the Scriptures, she was also fully aware of what was to come—the promised Messiah, the King who would save her and her people. God had been silent for four hundred years[11] but Mary had not mistaken His silence with unfaithfulness. Mary, along with all of her friends, I'm sure was eagerly anticipating His arrival and wondering who would be the one chosen to give birth to the promised Messiah.

At this point in Mary's life, she was engaged to Joseph. In those days a girl could get engaged (betrothed) around the time of puberty. It would generally last for twelve months. According to scholars, Mary was spending the last year of her life at home learning from her mother how to be a good wife and mother[11]. Her fiance, Joseph, was a good man. He was a hard-working carpenter and Mary was pleased her parents had made such a good choice for her. Then all of a sudden, as Mary is no doubt going about her day, the Angel Gabriel appeared to Mary to announce Christ's Birth.

> Now in the sixth month the angel Gabriel was sent by God to a city of Galilee named Nazareth, to a virgin betrothed to a man whose name was Joseph, of the house of David. The virgin's name was Mary. And having come in, the angel said to her, "Rejoice, highly favoured one, the Lord is with you; blessed are you among women!"
> But when she saw him, she was troubled at his saying, and considered what manner of greeting this was. Then the angel said to her, "Do not be afraid, Mary, for you have found favour with God. And behold, you will conceive in your womb and bring forth a Son, and shall call His name Jesus. He will be great, and will be called the Son of the Highest; and the Lord God will give Him the throne of His father David. And He will reign over the house of Jacob forever,

and of His kingdom there will be no end."

Then Mary said to the angel, "How can this be, since I do not know a man?"

And the angel answered and said to her, "The Holy Spirit will come upon you, and the power of the Highest will overshadow you; therefore, also, that Holy One who is to be born will be called the Son of God. Now indeed, Elizabeth your relative has also conceived a son in her old age; and this is now the sixth month for her who was called barren. For with God nothing will be impossible."

Then Mary said, "Behold the maidservant of the Lord! Let it be to me according to your word." And the angel departed from her. (Luke chapter 1 verses 26-38, NKJV)

Here we see Mary, a poor girl from an insignificant family, from a humble town chosen to be the mother of Jesus, the Virgin Mother, the second Eve. And Mary responds with a resounding yes; let it to be to me according to your word.

Mary said yes without knowing all of the details first.

Often we think and confess that we'll say yes to the plans, purposes and even God's promises when we have a detailed outline of how it will all play out; when we know how it will affect us when we know that it will work out well for us. However, if the life of Mary teaches us anything, it's that God uses the simple faith of a teenage girl to bring about His story. He chose her, divinely appointed her and she said yes. She said yes to not knowing all the details, but trusting that God did.

Mary had just found out that she was pregnant! I'm certain her next thoughts would be wondering: what would Joseph say about this?

> Now the birth of Jesus Christ was as follows: After His mother Mary was betrothed to Joseph, before they came together, she was found with child of the Holy Spirit. Then Joseph her husband, being a just man, and not wanting to make her a public example, was minded to put her away secretly. But while he thought about these things, behold, an angel of the Lord appeared to him in a dream, saying, "Joseph, son of David, do not be afraid to take to you Mary your wife, for that which is conceived in her is of the Holy Spirit. And she will bring forth a Son, and you shall call His name Jesus, for He will save His people from their sins."
> So all this was done that it might be fulfilled which was spoken by the Lord through the prophet, saying: "Behold, the virgin shall be with child, and bear a Son, and they shall call His name Immanuel," which is translated, "God with us."
> Then Joseph, being aroused from sleep, did as the angel of the Lord commanded him and took to him his wife, and did not know her till she had brought forth her firstborn Son. And he called His name Jesus. (Matthew chapter 1 verses 18-25)

Here, Joseph knows that Mary would have been a public example—according to scholars this is talking about the punishment of death by stoning. This was ordained by the Jewish law in such a case. As Mary is no doubt trying to work out what is going to happen with Joseph, we see God sorting and working it all out.

When we say yes to the big picture, God looks after the details.

> We can make our plans, but the LORD determines our steps. (Proverbs chapter 16 verses 9 NLT)

> The Lord directs the steps of the godly.
> He delights in every detail of their lives.
> (Psalm chapter 37 verses 23 NLT)

Too often we hold off on saying yes until we have all the details. And yet, what we often don't realise is that God is in our yes, sorting out the details.

After the Angel Gabriel appears to Mary and tells her that Elizabeth, who was also old and barren, is now six months pregnant, what is the first thing that Mary does? She runs to Elizabeth. Could you imagine Mary travelling all the way to the town of Hebron thinking, "Oh my, I wonder if it could be true? I wonder if Elizabeth is pregnant?"

Of course, when she arrived, everything the Angel had said was true. Elizabeth was indeed pregnant. And yet, how wonderful for Elizabeth—that God would use her as part of Mary's story. That she would be a sign to Mary that everything the Angel just told her is true! That Elizabeth's barrenness may have been changed for Mary's sake. That Mary's 'yes' would mean that Elizabeth's life changed as well.

When we say yes, our yes affects others.

I wonder what would have happened to Elizabeth if Mary hadn't said yes. You never know who your 'yes' will affect. But you saying 'yes' will affect another's life for the better.

Your 'yes' to being integrous in your workplace will affect others; your 'yes' to closing down gossip will affect your future relationships; your 'yes' to raising your children in the house of God will affect their future; your 'yes' to standing by the promises that He has given you will help so many.

Scripture then goes on to say that Mary found the courage to give birth to the promised Messiah. To bring heaven to Earth; to raise Jesus; to see her other children reject Jesus early in life; to see her Son be falsely accused and sentenced to death; to watch her own Son be cruelly nailed to a cross and hang there for hours; to watch on as He was crucified for her own sin. It certainly wasn't always pleasant, however Mary still said yes.

We say yes, we are saying yes to courage.

I'm sure Mary must have been feeling a little out of her comfort zone early on in life—being a teenager when the Angel appeared to her. And yet she remained courageous throughout her entire life.

In Luke chapter 1, verse 34 Mary asks how will I become pregnant? The Angel responds that a Divine power will undertake it, that she will be overshadowed by the Holy Spirit. Because Mary said 'yes', she became witness to something that she couldn't have ever possibly done on her own. It was only possible because of the power of the Holy Spirit.

When we say yes, we authorize the power of God in our lives.

I have found that at times I get a little too used to the routine; too accustomed to what happens in the natural. And then every now and then, God exceeds our natural expectations—it's like a gentle yet powerful reminder that God is at work in our lives, working for us and with us.
Luke chapter 1, verse 37 says:

> For with God nothing shall be impossible. (AMP)

Romans chapter 4, verses 20-21 reminds us that even Abraham had to trust that God was working out the details when the situation seemed impossible.

> Yet, with respect to the promise of God, he (Abraham) did not waver in unbelief but grew strong in faith, giving glory to God, and being fully assured that what God had promised, He was able also to perform. (NASB)

Matthew Henry, in his commentary on Luke chapter 1, says:

Abraham staggered not as the belief of the divine promise, because he was strong in his belief of the divine power.

Saying yes should authorize the power of God in our lives; in our expectations of what might happen—what God could do with our lives and those around us.

The only reason we know Mary's name, is because she said yes. Don't we all want some level of significance in life? Whether that's at least to be known by someone or for something. And yet, what we often don't realise is that this feeling of significance is tied to knowing Jesus and saying yes to His will in our lives. Mary would never have known the great example that she would be over 2000 years later, if she hadn't said yes in that moment.

When we say yes to Jesus, we are saying yes to significance.

What would Mary have done if she hadn't said yes? No doubt, she would have gone ahead and married Joseph and had children, but she would never have known Jesus in the way that only she ever could. Saying 'yes' brings incredible significance to our lives because our significance can only come from the One who created us.

At the very start of Luke chapter one, where the Angel Gabriel tells Mary that she will bear the promised King, Mary couldn't have possibly understood how exactly it was going to happen. But what I love about this is that Mary didn't need all the details—just a simple yes. We may look at this and think that saying 'yes' was just a once-off, but in reality it was the pattern of Mary's life.

What does God want from us at this particular point in our lives today? The same thing that He wanted from Mary—simple faith to say yes to the plans and purposes that He has for us and although we mightn't know all the details, nor be able to completely comprehend them, we trust that He certainly does.

The power of our yes has the ability to change our lives, just as it did for Mary.

Chapter 18

TRUST IN THE PROCESS

Let us not become weary in doing good, for at the proper time we will reap a harvest if we do not give up. (Galatians 6:9 NIV)

―――

I first heard these three words when we were going through our first and only round of in vitro fertilisation (IVF). Naturally, I was feeling a little exhausted from it all—emotionally and physically. We were about halfway through the process when someone close to me encouraged me to just trust the process. It was some of the best advice I had been given in this chapter of my life. Here we were doing all we possibly could to have another child when someone suddenly stopped me and reminded me that now I just needed to trust the process.

This meant that I needed to trust that our infertility specialist, with his 40 plus years of experience, knew what he was doing and that he had a detailed plan laid out just for us. I also needed to trust my body that it too would do exactly as it should in response to all that was taking place. Then of course I needed to trust God, that He would do exactly as He said He would and deliver on

His promise—whether it would be achieved this way or another. I had felt strongly led to go down this path, so I then had to trust God would deliver on His Word.

In the book of Matthew, chapter 27, we read of Pontius Pilot, the man who convicted Jesus of treason and ordered for him to be crucified. Jesus' crucifixion was a part of God's plan in Jesus becoming the Saviour of the world. Pontius Pilot was a part of the process, a very important one. Without Pontius Pilot, does Jesus still get crucified?

Sometimes we get so focused on the end goal we overlook the significance of each part of the process and the timing of it.

Trusting in the process isn't always easy. It means admitting that we are mere humans but that we have a powerful, almighty God who knows more and can see further than we can. It's being okay with the here and now yet being unsettled enough to believe God for more. It's trusting that God can and will use anything to achieve His ultimate purpose in our lives. And to live with a deep conviction of knowing that, when we do all we can, then He will come alongside of us and do all He can too.

In life we have to trust the process, that even better than an infertility specialist having a plan for us, our God has the greatest plan for us and our family.

I recently heard a preacher talk about the 'long play concept'; that we mustn't just be excited about the here and now, but we must be excited to be in this faith journey for the long haul.

Like a farmer who plants seed knowing that it may be years before he reaps a harvest, we too must embrace the here and now and trust that God will use everything for His purpose. That those deepest desires and dreams we have, will come to pass if we just stay the path and don't give up!

As we choose to trust the process, we too must remind ourselves and those around us that He's got it, that we're not to quit or give up too soon, that He has not forgotten you, to stop comparing, and to be grateful for each part, no matter how great or small. This part of your life is significant, so have faith and just trust where God has you.

You are right where you are meant to be.

Chapter 19

HOW'S YOUR FAITH?

He who promised is faithful. (Hebrews 10:23 NIV)

We are to experience God's goodness in our lives first hand. We aren't meant to just talk about it. His desire is that each and every single person would be able to taste and see that the Lord is good.

I'll never forget the moment when I thought I was pregnant with Sophie. It was the morning of August 13th, 2018, when I woke up with a vision of a double rainbow. Initially feelings of excitement and anticipation overwhelmed me, but I tucked the reminder of His promise away. A few days later I remembered, and began to question if I may actually be pregnant. I was blown away when I began to see two lines on the pregnancy test. We were about to start a new round of IVF literally the following week—it was a much more intense round of IVF but we had a plan in place. Yet, God clearly had something else in mind.

The very next day I was sent for bloods to confirm elevated HCG levels in my blood stream—something that my specialist wanted to monitor very closely. The results came back positive but rather low, yet I had this peace that this was it. The following two weeks consisted of more blood tests which really meant trusting in God's character, having patience, and also included some sleepless nights. But every time I would speak with the nurses from the specialists' clinic, they would tell me in absolute astonishment that my HCG levels were on the rapid rise. I had a confirmed positive pregnancy at the seven-week mark, which is where we really wanted to get to. I started crying happy tears over the phone and the nurse replied, "Yeah, what the! And you conceived naturally?"

We were seven weeks pregnant with all super positive hormone levels. God had turned our 'it's not impossible' situation into the grandest possibility. God was fulfilling His promise, prophecies that had been spoken of, and desires that we had had for some time now.

For three and a half years we had prayed, believed, waited and fought in the spiritual. Our family had sacrificed for us as we had too, in order to do all we could in the natural, and now to hear such wonderful news and those three words "you are pregnant" was nothing short of a miracle.

At the time I was reading a devotional by author and speaker Sheila Walsh on Psalm 136, where she used this—*Never, ever, ever forget all I have done for you.* It was in this moment when I realised I never ever wanted to forget this moment. I never wanted to forget the miracle that He was doing. Jesus really can do exceedingly more than we could ever ask, dream or imagine (Ephesians chapter 3, verse 20). Here I was thinking we were about to start another round of IVF the following week, but the miracle was already in motion.

Never, ever, ever will I forget that He chose to heal me. Never, ever, ever will I forget all that He has done for me.

> Let all that I am praise the LORD; may I never forget
> the good things he does for me.
> (Psalm chapter 103, verse 2 NLT)

May we never forget all He has done and continues to do.

Isn't it funny that, even when you receive your miracle, you still need to be as diligent in your thought life, if not more now than ever before. But God had spoken to me that this was the child we had prayed for (1 Samuel chapter 1, verse 27) and so we kept speaking that over this child.

Shortly after, we went for our dating scan. Our specialist began to look for our little bubba's sac. To our shock and utter devastation, he proceeded to say, "I'm so sorry guys but I'm going to wreck your afternoon... I can see a sac but there is no heartbeat." He began to explain that it may be a blighted ovum which would explain why all my blood level readings were positive. I began to cry and asked him if he was sure and to see if he would scan again. He agreed, saying he'll have one more look. I just knew, and so badly wanted him to be wrong.

Then, with great relief he said, "you're going to kill me, there it is, there's the sac and there's your baby. I was looking at the ovary that released the egg—your baby's heartbeat is great."

He repeatedly apologised and said that he hadn't made that mistake in a very long time. At the end of it all he said, "you'll be right now" meaning this baby will be right. We didn't need to see him anymore. I had dreamt of the day that we would drive off leaving his rooms because we were pregnant, and all of a sudden it was coming to pass.

Daniel and I went to grab something to eat, sit down and gather our thoughts. We were so relieved to see our little bub's heartbeat, especially after he couldn't find it. It was in that moment I thought—how's my faith? I felt so faith-filled and hopeful, as if anything was possible.

Then, on the 10th December 2018 during our 20 week scan, we finally heard those three beautiful words from the sonographer's mouth—It's a GIRL! God was fulfilling His promise. We were 20 weeks pregnant with our promised girl and she was perfect. I literally had tears running down my eyes for the remainder of the appointment, I couldn't stop them. We had told our sonographer what we had been through, but he had really no idea of the significance of that moment for us. I knew God was faithful, but witnessing it and experiencing it firsthand was something different all together.

Over the next few months, we continued to declare His goodness over our lives, we also were packing up our current townhouse to move into a much bigger home. God had been so good to us. The expectation I felt for this little girl and her future and the bond between her older brother and her at times overwhelmed me. I remember packing up the room where we had put the bassinet, her name sign that I had purchased more than two years earlier, and where we put different cards and little girl booties that very kind people had felt lead to buy us over the years. Times when I lacked the faith to continue believing, God prompted others to step in to remind and encourage me not to give up. I waited with such anticipation. There were moments when I wanted her to be born that very instant, so that I could finally hold her. But I realised that it was far better she stayed put until she was full term. I had waited this long, what was a few more weeks?

I had to learn to appreciate my body, to trust that it would do exactly what it was designed to do—carry a child. For the first time, I realised that her being in my womb was the safest place for her until she was due. That may sound simple and straightforward but that was a place that previously brought me much turmoil, angst and heartache.

We were about to enter a new season of new life, of faithfulness and fruitfulness. I was going to be a mother of two world changers.

If Jesus can conquer the grave, then He can certainly conquer anything that you and I are faced with.

How is your faith right now?

Chapter 20

SPOILS OF WAR

He will return the years that the locusts have eaten.
(Joel 2:25 NIV)

U.S. law defines the concept '**spoils of war**' as *"enemy movable property lawfully captured, seized, confiscated, or found which has become United States property in accordance with the laws of war."*

It applies to what belongs by right or custom to the victor in war or political contest.

When we go through a tough time and then walk out a victor, we take ground from the enemy. The enemy is very strategic in the way he attempts to distract, discourage and derail us. There is a reason why this even intensifies right before we achieve victory in that particular area of our lives. It is because he is fully aware that when we come out the victor, we have more authority, our faith has been enlarged and we have a deeper trust in God's character. We start to believe that perhaps all those other promises that God has given me will indeed come to fruition. Our prayer life even shifts as we really do believe that anything is possible. To me, these are spoils of war. When I see this promise come to pass I will have captured, seized, confiscated things back from the enemy.

> The enemy intended to harm me, but God intended it for good. (Genesis chapter 50, verse 20 NIV)

We all have spoils of war that we carry from one victorious season into the next. In life, people often use the term 'find the gold' in each and every season. And that is a good thing, but I prefer the term 'spoils of war' as it infers that when we get victory in one area of life, we walk away with more things in our pockets than just winning or overcoming in that area.

The term 'spoils of war' is not new. It was first mentioned in the Bible.

> The sons of Israel returned from chasing the Philistines and plundered their camps. (1 Samuel chapter 17 verse 53 AMP)

> When Jehoshaphat and his people came to take their spoil, they found much among them, including goods, garments and valuable things which they took for themselves, more than they could carry. And they were three days taking the spoil because there was so much. (2 Chronicles chapter 20 verse 25)

In Exodus chapter 4, we see God instruct Moses to return to Egypt. God warns Moses that He will harden Pharaoh's heart and that he will not let the people go, but encourages Moses to perform all the wonders before Pharaoh that He has given him the power to do so.

Consequently, after each plague that God sends, Moses goes to Pharaoh to try and negotiate with him. Each time Moses leaves with an option to go but with less than the best. Finally, after much negotiating and the final plague occurring, Pharaoh decides to let the Israelites go free—exactly 430 years to the day that they arrived. But after all this time, the Israelites didn't just walk out empty handed; they got their freedom that God had promised but they also received much more. Scripture says in Exodus chapter 12, verses 35-36 that the Israelites left with all the treasure of Egypt.

And this is exactly how our God works. In Joel chapter 2, verse 25 it says that He will return the years that the locusts have eaten. And not only that, but that we will reap where we haven't even sown (John chapter 4, verse 38). The Israelites are finally walking out, 430 years to the day, and not empty handed or worse off than they were before but with all of Egypt's precious gold and goods.

Spoils of war are the things that you carry out as a victor from the war. You may have been bruised, bloodied, hurt, scarred, scared or traumatised. But you walk out a victor with spoils—treats. When we go through a fight whether physically, mentally or emotionally, with our health, finance or relationships, and come out the other side a victor, we too can walk out with our own 'spoils of war.' Spoils of breakthrough, of greater trust, of greater understanding of God's character, greater confidence in our calling, greater determination in the promises that He has spoken over our life. These are our spoils of war, and we all have access to them. So often we walk out of poor situations, even when we have been victorious, and yet we are still focused on the bruises, the blood that was shed, the hurt, the scars and the trauma rather than focusing in on, and walking with, the spoils of war!

When I come out of a fight victorious, I want to walk out with all the good stuff.

I'm sure the enemy would love nothing more than to remind us of all the bad stuff that took place, to keep replaying that over rather than allowing us to enjoy the freedom that this victory brings. There lies the problem—we may *be* victorious, but we *remain* defeated. This is not how Jesus wants us to live. He wants us to be victorious and to live victoriously! I believe He wants us to look back at each season with gladness in our hearts. To walk out of awful seasons with a newfound strength and depth of relationship with Him.

I love it when I meet different people and, to be frank, I'm shocked as they tell me their story of the hard time they have been through, because you never would have known. They haven't lost their joy, they seemed happy and confident and clearly made a conscious decision to focus on the good from the situation. They don't deny that it is a part of their story, but they're clearly healed from it and have moved on. They've taken, stole back, captured something that the enemy had that was rightfully theirs and they weren't letting go.

I've had friends abused by perpetrators who easily could have gone on living with a victim mentality but instead they choose to take back that power. Something may have happened to them, but they decided not to go on living subservient to it. They've turned it around and

PROMISE KEEPER

actually used it for good to help others. I believe this is how God wants us to live and how He has always intended us to live—as victorious and overcomers! He not only wants us to inherit the promises that He has for us, but also to claim and fully receive our inheritance (Ephesians chapter 1, verse 11).

Chapter 21

NEW LIFE

We were therefore buried with him through baptism into death in order that, just as Christ was raised from the dead through the glory of the Father, we too may live a new life.
(Romans 6:4 NIV)

I prayed for this child, and the Lord has granted me what I asked of Him. (1 Samuel 1:27 NIV)

―――

At the beginning of each year I always ask God for a word for the year, for me personally, our family and our church. At the beginning of 2019, God spoke two words—New Life.

This made a lot of sense. We were finally moving into a home that we had been believing for and we were pregnant with our miracle girl. But God meant for so much more. Sophie's due date was the 29th April, but seeing as she was breeched, she was due to be delivered via caesarean on the 23rd April, two days after Easter Sunday. During the last seven weeks of my pregnancy,

I had been experiencing really strong Braxton Hicks Contractions so I had wondered if she would come early, but as time passed it didn't look like it. Then during the week leading up to Easter I had really bad back pain, I also felt like the Holy Spirit kept reminding me of the double rainbow He showed me the morning I 'knew' I was pregnant with her. It was like He was reminding me yet again, that this promise was about to come to pass. So, I was all packed and ready to go, just in case someone did decide to come a little earlier than expected.

With a big weekend celebrating Easter in church, we decided to take Jonathan out to breakfast on Saturday morning the 20th April. The next morning, Easter Sunday, Daniel would be preaching in church, so we figured it would be nice to have some time together as the next time we would have breakfast together we would be celebrating as a family of four! Thankfully, following breakfast, we had already arranged with my sister in law to look after Jonathan for a couple of hours so Daniel and I could spend some time together getting some last-minute things.

Poor Daniel, we were walking around the shopping centre and I was in such agony even walking. Then we would literally have to stop when the Braxton Hicks contraction would come on, firstly, because of how much pain I was in but also, so I could catch my breath—little did I know I was probably in the early stages of labour! Jonathan was also delivered via caesarean as he presented in a frank breach position. So, I had never experienced anything like this. Anyway, after a rather full day, we picked up Jonathan then grabbed some hot chips and headed home. Later that afternoon,

PROMISE KEEPER

I was on the phone to a good friend when the Braxton Hicks contractions started up again, however, this time they were even more intense and frequent. So, after I hung up the phone I decided to get out the timer and start timing them. Sure, enough they were consistent. Every 15-20 minutes it would happen again. I started realising, perhaps this little girl wants to come out now. So, I decided to do what you do when you start panicking—I scrubbed our bathroom with domestos (haha!) and told Dan to hurry up and pack his bag!

Over the next two hours, the contractions continued to occur every 15 minutes. They were intensifying, and as time went on, the time between them was reducing. So around 8pm in the evening, I called the hospital and told them what was happening. They had my file of course, and one of the beautiful nurses said, "Yeah, bub is breeched. We'd better get you up here straight away."

Of course, I called my parents to come and look after Jonathan. I had already called them to give them a heads up, but this time I said to them, "I think you had better come now".

As soon as my parents arrived we hurried to the hospital. Dan dropped Mum and I off at the front door and went to park. As Mum and I were walking into the reception, I had another really strong contraction and very well knew, after years of waiting, we may just be meeting our little Sophie tonight! It all happened pretty quickly from there.

We spoke to our obstetrician and, with things intensifying and really only a couple days away from the planned caesarean, our obstetrician asked, "well, do you want to have this baby tonight?" YES! I had waited a long time, yet was still in some disbelief that what we had waited so long and hard for was about to come to pass!

Within no time, I was sitting on the bed having my spinal block inserted by the anaesthetist, Daniel was praying, and Mum was helping me to stay calm. They told me that they were cutting, I felt some pulling and within moments Sophie entered the world with a big cry! Following her cry, I burst into tears—it was almost like a cry/yelp of relief that she was finally here, and she was safe in our arms. I sobbed; I just couldn't believe it.

Sophie Pearl Pappas entered the world at 10:58pm on Saturday, 20th April 2019 weighing 3900 grams, 48cm long and head circumference of 37cm with the most beautifully shaped red lips and the most stunning blue eyes and cheeks you cannot help but squeeze. She was, and is, perfect in every way. Sophie, meaning wisdom, and Pearl after my great grandmother, which also happens to be my middle name.

We welcomed in Easter Sunday—the very day that represents New Life. Celebrating the very person who brings new life into our lives, Jesus, the only one who can redeem and restore and turnaround anything—and we were now holding our little perfect Sophie girl. So many words had been spoken over my womb and our ability to have and carry another child, so many different diagnoses given, so much grief, yet Jesus brought life.

And not just life, but NEW life! God had fulfilled His promise to us and had given us our heart's desires and every time I look at her, I can't help but smile and think of how good He is!

Chapter 22

A CANVAS OF GRACE

The boundary lines have fallen for me in pleasant places; surely I have a delightful inheritance.
(Psalm 16:6 NIV)

So much can change in a short time period. After Daniel and I announced that we were pregnant, someone said to me—if only you could have showed a picture of your life now to yourself 12 months ago. I wonder what I would have said?

Jesus didn't have to give us another child, we didn't have to be rewarded this side of eternity for being faithful and standing on His Word, yet we were. But that's what grace is—we don't earn it and we certainly don't deserve it, yet God so freely gives it.

I titled this chapter 'A Canvas of Grace', because I truly believe that this is how Jesus wants us to see our lives, as if it were upon a canvas of grace. A canvas because it represents the great vastness of love that He has for us, but also because it has boundaries. I love the possibilities of a pure blank canvas. But I also love that it has borders, it is confined to a particular height and width.

David writes in Psalm chapter 24, verse 3 (MSG):

> Who can climb Mount God? Who can scale the holy north-face? Only the clean-handed, only the pure-hearted; men who won't cheat, women who won't seduce.

From the age of six I learnt to play the piano. I played a number of different piano pieces over the years. Generally, depending on the piano piece, you have to keep within a particular octave. This is where the melody sounds the best. If you play the entire piece or some of the keys in the next octave above or below you can still play it, but it doesn't sound anywhere near as good. It sounds best when you play according to the instructions. Our lives are much like this, if we live according to how God instructs us to live (Exodus chapter 20, verses 2-17) there seems to be a greater ease upon our lives and freedom. We can go on living outside of these commandments, but we won't be living in the same freedom perhaps we once were.

Romans chapter six, verses 4-6 (AMP):

> What shall we say, then? Shall we go on sinning so that grace may increase? By no means! We are those who have died to sin; how can we live in it any longer? Or don't you know that all of us who were baptized into Christ Jesus were baptized into his

death? We were therefore buried with him through baptism into death in order that, just as Christ was raised from the dead through the glory of the Father, we too may live a new life.

Paul is asking the very question—so what then, can we go on sinning so that grace may abound all the more? No, he responds, by no means! We all need boundaries in our lives, to live within, as a framework for our life.

When I was a young girl, my mother encouraged me to learn Mark chapter 11 verse 25—to ask Jesus for forgiveness for my sins. Even as a young girl I learnt to repent of my sins and ask for God's forgiveness. I desired to live a life that was holy (as much as I could). I could have practiced it a lot more through my teenage years. But I always desired to have a healthy fear of God.

I have seen people receive tremendous blessing upon their lives whilst living within these boundaries, I've also seen people receive blessing while they haven't been, but sin always has a way of catching up with you.

Just like children work better with discipline, so do we as adults. We all need wisdom, counsel, guidance, rules and discipline because without it we simply can go wayward. We begin to move away from this canvas of grace.

When I was in Bible college, our Associate Pastor became famous for his teaching on the pendulum. He would teach us that life experiences, beliefs and perspectives would swing us one way or the next, but the best place that we could find ourselves is fixed right in the centre, based on the truth of God's Word. The Word of God is our compass.

In the Old Testament, people had to atone for their sins every year. Yet Jesus came to fulfil the law. His desire for us today is to continue living in righteousness, this is still His plan for all of humanity. To live within a canvas of grace. We can achieve this by repenting of our sins, asking for Jesus's forgiveness and if we have never made Jesus the Saviour of our life then we can do so by inviting him into our life.

What was most important to me, even more than receiving the promises our God had for us here on Earth, was my relationship with Him.

Wherever you find yourself today, why don't you pray this simple, yet powerful prayer and invite Jesus into your life. Perhaps you have prayed this prayer before but haven't been living for God, then right now why don't you pray this out loud. And I will believe with you that you will never be the same again as every day you choose to honour him in your life.

Dear God,
I recognise that I need you
God I ask you
To forgive me of all of my mistakes
Wash my heart completely clean
I thank you that you love me
That you proved it
When Jesus died on the cross for me
From this moment on
I want to live for you
I want to be a Christian
In Jesus name, AMEN.

PROMISE KEEPER

As I sit here and pen the final words of this book, my baby girl sits and stares up at me—this little girl whom Jesus promised. Not a day goes by where I am not utterly thankful to Jesus for her.

APPENDICES

A declarative prayer for first or secondary infertility:

Jesus I thank you that you love me.
I thank you that your Word says that none shall be barren or miscarry. I thank you that your Word never returns void and so today I command that my body would come into alignment with your Word. I receive your promises in Jesus name. Amen.

KEY Scriptures:

> I praise you because I am fearfully and wonderfully made; your works are wonderful, I know that full well. (Psalm 139:14 NIV)

> We walk by faith, not by sight. (2 Corinthians 5:7 NIV)

> ...so is my word that goes out from my mouth: It will not return to me empty, but will accomplish what I desire and achieve the purpose for which I sent it. (Isaiah 55:11 NIV)

The Lord's promises are pure, like silver refined in a furnace, purified seven times over. (Psalm 12:6 NLT)

Every word of God is flawless; He is a shield to those who take refuge in Him. (Proverbs 30:5 NIV)

We do not want you to become lazy, but to imitate those who through faith and patience inherit what has been promised. (Hebrews 6:12 NIV)

So cheer up! Take courage all you who love Him. Wait for Him to breakthrough for you, all who trust in Him. (Psalm 31:24 TPT)

See, I am doing a new thing! Now it springs up; do you not perceive it? I am making a way in the wilderness and streams in the wasteland. (Isaiah 43:19 NIV)

Instead of shame and dishonour, you will enjoy a double share of honour.
You will possess a double portion of prosperity in your land, and everlasting joy will be yours. (Isaiah 61:7 NIV)

For the vision awaits an appointed time. (Habakkuk 2:3 NIV)

Then Peter said, "Silver or gold I do not have, but what I do have I give you. In the name of Jesus Christ of Nazareth, walk." (Acts 3:6 NIV)

He has given me a new song to sing, a hymn of praise

to our God. Many will see what he has done and be amazed. They will put their trust in the Lord. (Psalm 40:3 NIV)

That is why I am suffering as I am. Yet there is no cause for shame, because I know whom I have believed and am convinced that he is able to guard what I have entrusted to him until that day. (2 Timothy 1:12 NIV)

And none will miscarry or be barren in your land. I will give you a full life span. (Ezekiel 23:26 NIV)

With man this is impossible, but with God all things are possible. (Matthew 19:26 NIV)

You are the God who performs miracles; you display your power among the peoples. (Psalm 77:14 NIV)

...for He who promised is faithful. (Hebrews 10:23 NIV)

I prayed for this child, and the Lord has granted me what I asked of him. (1 Samuel 1:27 NIV)

He will return the years that the locusts have eaten (Joel 2:25 NIV)

The boundary lines have fallen for me in pleasant places; surely I have a delightful inheritance. (Psalm 16:6 NIV)

Psalm 24 (TPT) The Glorious King

David's poetic praise to God

God claims the world as his. Everything and everyone belongs to him!

He's the one who pushed back oceans to let the dry ground appear, planting firm foundations for the earth. Who, then, ascends into the presence of the Lord? And who has the privilege of entering into God's Holy Place?

Those who are clean—whose works and ways are pure, whose hearts are true and sealed by the truth, those who never deceive, whose words are sure.

They will receive the Lord's blessing and righteousness given by the Saviour-God.

They will stand before God, for they seek the pleasure of God's face, the God of Jacob. Pause in his presence. So wake up, you living gateways!

Lift up your heads, you ageless doors of destiny! Welcome the King of Glory, for he is about to come through you.

You ask, "Who is this Glory-King?"

The Lord, armed and ready for battle, the Mighty One, invincible in every way!

So wake up, you living gateways, and rejoice!
Fling wide, you ageless doors of destiny!

Here he comes; the King of Glory is ready to come in.
You ask, "Who is this King of Glory?"

He is the Lord of Victory, armed and ready for battle, the Mighty One, the invincible commander of heaven's hosts!

Yes, he is the King of Glory! Pause in his presence.

NOTES

Chapter 4

[1] https://www.endometriosisaustralia.org/about-endometriosis

Chapter 5

[2] http://www.baby-names-and-stuff.com/italian-baby-names/arabella.asp
[3] https://nameberry.com/babyname/Arabella
[4] https://healthengine.com.au/info/beta-hcg-test
[5] https://www.sands.org.au/miscarriage
[6] https://uscfertility.org/5-things-know-recurrent-miscarriages/
[7] https://uscfertility.org/5-things-know-recurrent-miscarriages/

Chapter 8

[8] http://english.oxforddictionaries.com/perseverance
[9] https://dictionary.cambridge.org/dictionary/english/patience

Chapter 9

[10] http://english.oxforddictionaries.com/holding%20pattern

Chapter 17

[11] https://bible.org/seriespage/lesson-10-mary-most-blessed-women

ABOUT THE AUTHOR

Elise Pappas is a pastor with the Australian Christian Churches, formerly AOG in Australia.

Elise has a genuine love for God and people. She has a kindness and gentleness that draws others in a natural way to Jesus wherever they may be in their life journey. She is energised to win souls for Christ.

On a quiet, cold, rainy day Elise can be found wrapped in God's Word, warmed by a love that is deep and earnest, unfolding in complexity and saturated so lovingly as only a Promise Keeper and King can be.

You can find Elise Pappas online at:
- www.awakenleadership.online
- instagram.com/awakenleadership
- facebook.com/Elise Pappas

CPSIA information can be obtained
at www.ICGtesting.com
Printed in the USA
LVHW112138160920
666201LV00001B/216

9 780648 460244